Rookie Dad

Rookie Dad

Thoughts on First-Time Fatherhood

David Jacobsen

ZONDERVAN®

ZONDERVAN.com/
AUTHORTRACKER
follow your favorite authors

Rookie Dad
Copyright © 2007 by David Jacobsen

Requests for information should be addressed to:

Zondervan, *Grand Rapids, Michigan 49530*

Library of Congress Cataloging-in-Publication Data

Jacobsen, David, 1977–
      Rookie dad : thoughts on first-time fatherhood / David Jacobsen.
         p.   cm.
      ISBN-13: 978-0-310-27921-1
      ISBN-10: 0-310-27921-6
      1. Fatherhood. 2. Fathers. 3. Father and child. I. Title.
   HQ756.J33   2007
   306.874'20971133 — dc22

2007027368

All rights reserved. No part of this publication may be reproduced, stored in
a retrieval system, or transmitted in any form or by any means — electronic,
mechanical, photocopy, recording, or any other — except for brief quotations in
printed reviews, without the prior permission of the publisher.

Author's note: Some of the descriptive details in this book have been changed
for reasons of privacy.

Interior design by Beth Shagene

Printed in the United States of America

---

07 08 09 10 11 12 13 • 20 19 18 17 16 15 14 13 12 11 10 9 8 7 6 5 4 3 2 1

For Christine and Nicholas:
finding our place in the family of things

• • •

Contents

Stage Fright

This week Christine stopped taking birth control. Although we'd discussed it at great length beforehand, the actual event felt like a headlong rush toward the edge of a cliff. I could be a father soon — very soon — and I'm terrified!

Terror sharpens my focus. I've thought up quite a weighty list of reasons against having a baby right now. I tick them off: I'm trying to get through grad school quickly, and a baby will slow me down; I need to focus on my studies; Christine and I are making less than we're spending right now; more years in school means more student loans to pay back later; having an American baby in Canada will be a paperwork nightmare; our parents live fifteen hundred miles away; wouldn't it be better to wait until we have more money, more space, and more stability?

Then there are the personal questions, the ones rooted deep inside me. Will my wife still love me as much after we have a baby? I feel like I'm finally starting to develop a solid friendship with my dad; don't I deserve more time to explore and learn from that relationship before becoming a father myself? How will my largely selfish and independent lifestyle be changed by a little person who is totally dependent on me? Will I be a good father?

So why, then, are we trying to have a baby? Why am I running on my own two legs toward the cliff's edge?

One night before Christine and I left our home in California to go to school in Vancouver, Dad and I went out to grab some pizza and beer. He had a Santa Barbara Blonde—a brew that's been the source of a few jokes—and I had a Mission Ale, choosing for myself the cloistered life. We waited for our pepperoni pizzas to arrive before talking about the future; having something to do lets us speak more easily about difficult things. I told him Christine and I wanted to start a family soon, and he asked if it might be better to wait. Struggling to justify our decision, I finally told my dad that Christine is fully alive when she is caring for a child. I told him that I want whatever makes my wife the most joyful and fulfilled, what makes her the most human. Around kids, I said, she absolutely shines.

That image of light returned to me recently. Walking down the stairway at school, I followed a young father holding his baby on his shoulder. As we descended, the baby made eye contact with me and a smile lit up his face. I smiled back. He blinked at each step, and after each blink, his shining eyes locked on mine. I couldn't take my eyes off of his. Maybe he liked my shirt or my hair; maybe he simply liked looking into my eyes. I imagined my own child in his face, and the contact delighted me. The rest of the day, remembering his toothless grin took the edge off my fear.

Having a baby isn't all bright eyes and smiles, though. I still find a troubling persistence in my questions about the wisdom of having a baby right now. It's true that Christine is ready to have a baby—and the sooner the better from her point of view. This is where another reason becomes clear: Christine's readiness carries me along, even though I'm not sure on my own of our destination. I trust Christine. This isn't too hard because I live with her; I watch the decisions she makes and the integrity with which she makes them. I believe that she's moving toward a place of growth and goodness, and I'm content to follow her.

This kind of trust is anything but blind. It simply takes now as its object of vision instead of then, and here in the now, things are pretty clear. In walking toward fatherhood, I am choosing a path perpendicular to selfishness. It won't, I know, be an easy path. Most of my questions can't be answered on this side of fatherhood anyway. While being a dad will provide some answers, I'm sure it will provide new and better questions.

Parents want to give the things they never had to their children. But giving new things seems like the easy part. The trick for me will be to give my child those things I *did* have. How will I pass on the love and care that have shaped me from birth, and shape me still? How will I continue the love story my parents are still writing? Writing is terrifying, but the writer must settle into the work of filling page after page. Soon, perhaps, I'll be ready to begin my own chapters: stories of sleepless nights and tear-filled days; stories of daily routine; stories of lying with my baby on my chest, watching my breath stir translucent hair, and tracing my finger in amazement around ears the size of buttons.

Ultrasound

Men have it rough when it comes to pregnancy. We take the whole thing on faith, without the constant confirmation of someone kicking our innards. There were times I wondered whether Christine could be making up her pregnancy, perhaps so that she could send me on late-night runs to Dairy Queen for Brownie Batter Blizzards.

Hearing the fetal heartbeat almost convinced me that this was for real. At thirteen weeks, the fetus is only the size of a jumbo shrimp and weighs just one ounce. When our doctor pointed the microphone at the precise spot, I heard a sound emerge from the background noise of Christine's abdomen: a rapid *PEE-oo PEE-oo PEE-oo* repeating at the fantastic rate of one hundred fifty beats per minute. Still, when Christine and I left the office, it was easy for me to forget that sound, to forget that there was a person inside of Christine whose heart was beating like a marathon runner's.

It wasn't until we went for our second ultrasound that my doubt finally dissolved. Our first ultrasound revealed a baby that looked like a cross between a jelly bean and an alien. The second ultrasound, I was told, would be much different. We didn't know what to expect, but we did hope to find out whether our baby was a boy or a girl. I wanted to be able to assign the grammatically correct pronoun to our baby, and Christine was anxious to start planning the appropriate wardrobe, nursery furniture, and names. In Vancouver, though, the technicians don't reveal the sex of the baby before twenty weeks because of the high incidence of sex-based abortions, and our appointment was scheduled at nineteen and a half weeks. Would they still tell us? Could we convince them to bend the rules?

The receptionist ordered Christine to drink a ridiculous amount of water—half a gallon—in the hour before the ultrasound, and she wasn't allowed to go to the bathroom. Christine took her place in the semicircle of pained, overhydrated women who were trying simultaneously to keep drinking and keep from peeing, like contestants on a crazy Japanese game show. We hoped that this was the sort of doctor's office that would see patients at their appointment time.

Christine managed to make it into the examining room without bursting. The lights were off, but a soft, gray glow shone from the ultrasound monitor. Normally, doctors leave you alone in their office for twenty minutes at a time, with nothing better to do than play with the blood pressure pump and steal tongue depressors and cotton balls. Since you're in your underwear, the doctors can be confident that you won't bolt for the door with an armful of prescription samples. In this office, alone in the dark with strange glowing monitors, we moved as little as possible and spoke in whispers. The ultrasound machine, with its power to see inside of us, silently controlled the room.

Christine laid back on the examining table while the technician smeared clear gel across her stomach. The technician turned on the monitor and began to probe with the ultrasound wand, using it like an extension of her own hand and fingers, pushing and searching for just the right spot. Quite a bit of prodding goes into an ultrasound, since one's internal landscape is sometimes camera shy and the technician needs to come at certain parts from certain angles. She began to give us a guided tour of Christine's lower abdomen—*here's your uterus, and this is the placenta, right here next to the umbilical cord*—like a guide pointing out notable sights in a national park. I began to suspect that she was making things up, since the screen looked like nothing but a mass of swirling, shapeless fog. *Oh, and here's that set of car keys you lost last year!* Why had people been telling me so many good things about this ultrasound?

I once stood in front of one of those optical illusions in which a three-dimensional shape will emerge from a chaotic background if one's eyes are crossed and focused just right. I stared and stared, seeing nothing, when all at once a sailboat rose from the surface of the poster and filled my vision. The ultrasound was something like that. Suddenly, like a shiver, a human shape materialized out of the white-and-black fuzz. It was like being in a crowded room, absentmindedly scanning the faces in the crowd, only to be startled to find the face of someone you know looking right into your eyes. Shapeless forms, and then—I caught my breath—our baby!

I was shocked to see that this person seemed to be acting much as I would in a similar situation. I know that comparing a fetus to an adult isn't very accurate—*look, dear, it's waving to us!*—but I felt like I understood what it was doing. It stretched its legs out, uncrossing and unfolding them as far as Christine's womb allowed. I saw myself sitting at a study cubicle in the college library, uncrossing my legs and stretching as far as I can after a long day of studying. Then, as if that stretch had accomplished its goal, our fetus returned to its original, well, fetal position and curled into a ball the size of a grapefruit.

The next ten minutes or so we watched as parts of our baby appeared on the screen and vanished. The gaze of the ultrasound saw right through its body, peering past bones and into the head and heart. It's a strange thing to look so closely and intimately at another person while remaining anonymous oneself. We could see the baby's mouth, nose, fingers, and toes, but we also stared at its brain, heart, and spine. This is a type of knowledge that is possible only before birth, before the skin matures and becomes opaque, and before a parent's knowledge of the inner workings of their child turns from photographic to empathetic.

Before the appointment, we knew that finding out the baby's sex might be problematic, given that we were a few days before the twenty-week deadline. Plan A was to act nice, keep our ears and eyes open, and hope that the technician would tell us on her own. As the appointment wrapped up without any indication of the baby's sex, we moved to Plan B.

"Do you see anything that would tell us if it's a boy or a girl?" asked Christine. The technician checked the fetal age—nineteen and a half weeks—and told us that she couldn't reveal the sex of the baby until after twenty weeks. Something in the tone of her voice suggested that we might still have a chance, though. Plan B was to convince her to bend the rules for us, mostly because we were so adorable.

"Aw, if only we'd known, we could have scheduled our appointment for next week instead!" said Christine.

I joined in, noting that the twenty week mark was nearly upon us; maybe we could just round up the age. The technician looked at us, and then she turned her attention to the monitor as she began moving the ultrasound probe across Christine's stomach. Christine and I could guess what was happening, but we didn't want to jinx things, so we shut up, held hands, and stared at the monitor.

This was the moment when I knew that I wanted our baby to be a boy, since in my head I was rooting for the technician to *find a penis, find a penis!* I held my breath, thinking that I might recognize the image on the screen. Abruptly, she pulled her instrument away from Christine's abdomen and shut off the machine. She turned to look at us. "You know I can't officially tell you the sex of the baby," she said, "but if you're thinking about painting the baby's room this weekend, if I were you, I'd use blue." She quickly left the room, and Christine and I squeezed each other's hand while we stared at the ultrasound screen, now empty. We had just seen our son. When we left the office, it felt, for the first time, like there were three of us.

That night, as Christine and I lay in bed, we talked in the dark about our son—now we could call him that! Had we really known all along that he would be a boy? Would he be blessed with Christine's teeth or cursed with mine? As our conversation slowed, we snuggled closer to each other. Christine moved her feet so that they were touching my legs underneath the blankets. I thought of our baby inside Christine's womb, stretching his legs to their full, tiny length, surrounded by the touch of his mother's body. Our son was already reaching, at every moment, for what he needed most.

The Odyssey

My father-in-law, Doug, drove our U-Haul truck through Oregon's snowy southern passes, using skills honed by countless hours at the wheel of his avocado-and-white RV, while I followed at a safe distance in my Honda Accord sedan. Well into the second day of our move from Santa Barbara, California, to Vancouver, British Columbia, my job was to follow Doug's lead and monitor our two-way radio for important messages from the truck, like warnings about ice on the road or groan-worthy jokes.

Three months earlier, Christine and I had decided to drive our belongings to our new home in Canada, an idea that was easier said (in a coffee shop over warm lattes) than done (in a U-Haul and a car across fifteen hundred miles of wet or icy highway). We did have the foresight to understand the boredom we'd face if we each drove a vehicle alone: flipping between country-western and Spanish radio stations, counting how many cars passed us per hour, and fending off sleep with no one to help. Besides, we think SUVs are too big to drive, never mind a moving van. We figured a rotating cast of drivers would be ideal. Anyone can become annoying when you spend three days driving together, but the threat of boredom was far worse. Christine's dad and her sister, Lisa, were happy to join us when we asked, and we were happy to have them. Lisa is gentle, tells great stories, and enjoys silly games. Doug is a guy who Knows Stuff, like what a carburetor is, the rules of poker, and how toilets flush. We had, without a doubt, the perfect driving team.

All that remained, after packing, was to leave. I remember three images from the afternoon we left. In the first, I'm sitting on my parents' couch in Santa Barbara on New Year's Day. Football is on television, friends and family are on couches, and steaming bowls of chili are on people's laps. I eat, and watch, and look at my family and friends, and think, *In a few hours, they'll still be here, and I'll be driving away to live in a new country.*

In the second image, I'm driving up my folks' cul-de-sac at fifteen miles per hour in warm, sunny weather, wincing as a hideous grinding and clanking comes from beneath my car. Doug and I had just finished installing the snow chains for practice — *If you can do it here, you just might be able to do it in the snow at night, right?* — and now I'm making sure they don't fall off as

I drive. Neighborhood kids screech their bikes to a halt and gawk, and I'm hunching down in the driver's seat, trying to be inconspicuous.

The third image is more like a sketch than a movie. I'm standing in the driveway, and everyone in the house has come outside to see us leave. Faces that I know and love seem to appear and disappear as I turn in a circle. Everyone is talking, everyone is moving. Whom do I hug? To whom do I say goodbye? I hug my mom, and my brother, Rick, and his wife, Kate. Rick shivers in the sun as he fights the flu. My dad gives me one of his familiar sideways hugs, his shoulders and head turning away as I wrap my arms around him. And then I'm suddenly in the street, sitting high in the cab of the U-Haul, waving goodbye as we pull away.

For Christmas, Christine and I decided to buy a pair of two-way radios for Doug, and then ask him to bring his present on our trip. While perhaps poor etiquette, this was right up Doug's alley: cool gadgets with an immediate use. Although indispensable for many practical reasons during our trip, the radios were most often used for conversations like this one:

"Are you guys there?"

"Yep."

"What kind of fish makes a living fixing pianos?"

"Uh, we don't know. We give up."

"You're sure you give up?"

"Yes. What's the answer?"

"You're sure you're ready?"

"Yes!"

"A tuna."

Our radio chatter took a turn for the serious as the weather deteriorated in northern California and throughout Oregon and Washington; we spent less time cracking wise and more time discussing the road conditions, often at great length.

"Ah, I think this corner is going to be a little icy, so go slow."

"Okay, got it."

"We're through the corner ... It felt fine, but take it slow anyway."

"Okay."

"How was that corner?"

"Fine."

"Alright, I was just checking. Y'know, you stop paying attention for just a second and it's like, 'Holy Cats! Where'd that ice come from!' Right?"

"Right."

"Okay, it looks like there might be another icy corner coming up ..."

We arrived in Vancouver eventually, late on the third night, happy to finally park the truck. The trip was sufficiently troublesome that Doug dubbed it "The Odyssey of '04," and the four of us did feel a sense of shared accomplishment. Some of our adventures will go down in family lore. As Interstate 5 leaves California and climbs into the Siskiyou Mountains, we found ourselves installing chains on both the car and the van. When I say "we," I mean us men. This was logical enough, since Doug and I had practiced just a few days earlier. And he was right: struggling with icy chains in the snow was a whole different experience. Semis chunked by us with their industrial-strength chains, scaring the pants off me as I knelt only a few feet away. Other drivers seemed to be getting their chains on much faster than we were. Once we manhandled the chains onto the van tires, a process involving trial, error, and four-letter words, we came back to put the chains on the Honda, in which Christine and Lisa were sitting. Needing to restore some feeling in my fingers, I knocked on the window, and Lisa rolled it down. I put my hands in front of the heater vent, and as I did so I saw that Christine and Lisa were knitting. I tried not to let this bother me. After all, I was happy to serve them graciously by kneeling in the icy slush and installing the chains. I did feel the teeniest bit put out, though, when they mentioned that with the window down, I was letting all the warm air out of the car.

Just outside of Tacoma, the highway was completely white, an unsettling experience for a Southern Californian. It was snowing steadily, and as evening approached, visibility continued to worsen. We passed car after car that had spun out and was now stuck in the snow on the side of the highway, headlights pointing at odd angles to the road or up into the air. Not wanting to join them, we pulled off the highway and into the parking lot of a pizza joint. We sat inside, huddled around a cold table, trying to keep the fear at bay. *Round Table Pizza, huh? Then why are all the tables square?* I went to use the restroom to avoid the debate between meat and veggies, and as I stood in that silent room, I realized that I felt, beyond the fear, a sense of protection. Doug was watching out for us, and we'd be able to handle whatever came up, together.

We did indeed make it to Vancouver late that night, to a new home that felt like anything but. After we pulled in, we discovered that the padlock on the back door of the truck was frozen shut. We managed to get the door open, with the help of our landlord's electric teapot, and found that while we'd had the foresight to pack our mattresses near the door, our pillows and blankets were buried all the way up near the cab. I stared at the contents of the truck, arms crossed and feet shuffling. The freezing air crystallized my sigh. Then Doug grabbed a box and headed for the house. Christine grabbed a bag full of shoes. Before long—you work fast when you're hunting for blankets in subzero weather—the four of us were inside for the night, warming beneath our comforters as snow fell outside.

Doug and I know that we're quite different. But spending hours together in a U-Haul is a great conversation starter, and we learned more about each other in those three days than we had in the previous three years. I learned a lot from watching, too. I saw him patiently unpacking snow chains for the second time in one day. I saw him calmly buying us hot pizza when we were scared and stressed—*I figure the highway'll open again soon ... We'll make it to Vancouver tonight.* I watched him love his family for seventy-two hours straight, giving me both a gift and something to live up to. As he was leaving, he wrapped me in one of his bear hugs and told me that he loved me. I realized that Doug and I had made it through our first three years together with a certain kind of love, the off-the-shelf variety that accompanies becoming a new family, the kind that thinks it might be easier if we were more alike. It was real love, but not very realistic. Now, a new kind of love was beginning to grow between us: a love that doesn't work around the differences, but works because of them.

Hiking

When I was twenty-five, I took my dad on a father-son camping trip. This was no day-hike, sleep-in-a-cabin jaunt but a manly, four-night, carry-our-own-food, crap-in-the-woods kind of trip through the Hoover Wilderness where Nevada nestles into the crook of central California. I had hiked the same route several years earlier while studying in southern Oregon, and I wanted to share some of that experience with my dad, who had made the wilderness a part of my life as I grew up.

One of the earliest memories I have is of hiking up the dirt fire-road to Henninger Flats north of Pasadena in the San Gabriel Mountains. Henninger Flats is a wilderness hike in the same way that George Bush is a president: only good enough to trick those who don't know any better. I was four and willingly and magnificently fooled. As far as I was concerned, we were about to *climb a mountain*, and I was pretty sure the top was *covered in trees!* At each switchback, I earned an M&M,

but even chocolate wasn't enough to keep my short legs pumping. Near the top, Dad lifted me onto his back, and I rode there, my arms draped around his neck and my legs wrapped around his sides. I felt the steady movement of his muscles and joints beneath his sweaty T-shirt, his body wiry and still able to fit into his Navy uniform (as he was, and still is, fond of reminding us).

Hiking was part of our family's culture. Summer trips to Oregon and Washington always included stops along the way to hike and explore, from the dusty top of volcanic Mount Lassen in northern California to the oddly inverted experience of hiking down to lake level at Crater Lake in southern Oregon. We also relaxed in nature, skipping rocks by lake's edge and clambering alongside streams and waterfalls. Nature wasn't something to be conquered, but was something to glory in. After hiking to the bottom of the Grand Canyon and back in one day, we felt less like conquerors and more like survivors. As we wearily untied our hiking boots back at the trailhead, the canyon maintained its ancient place in the order of things, turning violet and breathing its daytime heat into the inky night sky.

I first saw the Grand Canyon when I was ten. I was playing my Gameboy for about the tenth straight hour when we pulled into the parking lot at Mather Point. I dutifully switched off my game machine and loped down the path to the edge of the canyon. My eyes were on the rocky trail, and I reached the railing at the very edge of the canyon before I looked up. It was like a giant hand threw me into the canyon and then caught me in midair, and I felt safe and scared at the same time. It was like my whole being exhaled the words *My God* with as much meaning and faith as I've ever given them. It was like the pink-purple-orange kaleidoscope of sky and canyon slapped me in the face with its otherness. It was like I was awake for the first time. I breathed in; I breathed out. And the canyon was still there.

If there was a peak to be climbed on our vacation route, chances were that my brother and dad had already climbed it. Rick had a five-year head start on me, and the injustice galled me. As a five-year-old, I wondered, Why shouldn't I go on a steep, fifteen-mile hike? But each hike came to me in its own time, and I was no less thrilled to reach the top for having reached it third. I remember seeing a picture when I was small: Dad is perched near the top of South Sister in central Oregon, elevation 10,358 feet. It looks like the slope of the caldera is approaching a forty-five degree angle, and the trail is nothing more than a jumble of volcanic rocks. My father is sitting above the clouds.

Each evening, though, after hiking—Storm King, the Bright Angel Trail, Klamath Falls—we returned to the car, to a cabin, to a lovely log-and-mortar lodge in a national park. With a mom who didn't enjoy camping waiting for us at the trailhead, we couldn't stay in the wilderness overnight. So I grew up encountering nature in digestible, day-sized bites. The bar graph on the back of my Boy Scout newsletter showed the number of nights the various boys had spent camping: it sloped steeply upward like a mountain. At the peak was an Eagle Scout with over one hundred nights, while back at the parking lot was me, with one night.

So I planned our trip, ready to experience a deeper version of our childhood hikes, hoping to give back to my dad some of what he had given to me. It was also a way to create a huge chunk of father-son bonding time. A counselor I knew told me that the trip would be a perfect chance to talk to my dad, since we would be in the car together for six hours, not to mention on the trail for days. The counselor wasn't a hiker, and so she didn't understand that we wouldn't have much spare oxygen for talking once we started, and that what air we had would be reserved for the outdoor equivalent of guys talking about sports: *See that peak? Yeah. Amazing, huh? Yeah, amazing.* She had a point about the car, though, I had to admit. But still. What am I supposed to do, I asked her, wait until we're on the freeway and then ask Dad why he never talked to me about sex or dating or masturbation or pornography? Pretty much, she said, but you might want to lock the doors first.

We didn't talk about any of that during the car ride, but we did have time that belonged to just the two of us. No mom, no brother, no headphones or Gameboys. Just us, our map of California, buckets of coffee, and four hundred fifty miles of highway. We had the time and space to speak leisurely and enjoy each other. We listened to old episodes of *Prairie Home Companion* and laughed together at families that were just as awkward as ours was.

We reached the trailhead, parked, and began to hike. A California brown bear padded through the pine needles just off the trail to our right, paralleling our track for a while before snuffling off into the undergrowth. As the trail steepened and we felt the weight of our thirty-five-pound packs, our bodies began to complain. But as the day wore on, we found a rhythm of movement and rest, of snack breaks and scenic views. The first night, camping on the rocky shores of Peeler Lake, we found ourselves engulfed in clouds of mosquitoes. We ate a hasty dinner, sealed ourselves into our tent, and hoped that we wouldn't need to pee. The next day, we headed for ground that was higher and drier, and hopefully mosquito free. Our route took us along Rancheria Creek, which wanders and wends its way through a valley carpeted in small white and lavender wildflowers, before turning uphill toward Rock Island Pass and its tiny lake, where we spent the next night.

Waking to sore bodies, clear skies, and no mosquitoes, we decided to stay at the lake for a whole day. Why rush things? We had plenty of good food to eat, the kind of dehydrated fare that would barely seem edible at home, yet tastes like a feast when you're on the trail. We could walk around the lake, shoot the breeze, cook food, pack, and be ready to continue onward the following day. This lake wasn't even named on our map, and we came to think of it as our own private outpost.

For lunch, we both ate double our usual rations, knowing that the extra weight in our stomachs wouldn't hinder our afternoon plans for napping in the sun and poking around the lake. No five-star chef in the world could prepare better dishes than we did that afternoon: the deliciousness of dehydrated turkey stew with instant potatoes can't be topped when you eat them above ten thousand feet. We talked, and ate, and watched the wind ruffle the surface of the lake. And finally we had a personal conversation.

I asked Dad, "Do you ever have trouble with that?"

"Of course, like most guys."

"You do?"

"Yeah."

"Oh. That's good to know."

That was pretty much it. And it was enough. In these few words, I heard this: we're both men now, and even though we won't talk about this often, we both understand that the other is human. There were other things that I wanted to say, but not just then. In the silence, the Mountaintop Blueberry Crumble burbled on the camp stove. I cautiously pulled it off the heat. I slopped our steaming dessert into two mugs and took one over to Dad, who was looking out across the lake. "Careful, it's hot," I said, as he took his mug and I sat beside him. We watched the shadows cast by the clouds flow down the hill to our left and glide across the surface of the lake with the effortless ease of pelicans skimming the surf. The pass was quiet. We blew on our spoons, savoring the syrupy smell of the berries. The fruit tasted fantastic. I looked at Dad. "Nice job," he said.

Later that afternoon I hiked to the top of that same ridge. I looked north to the section of backcountry through which we'd hiked the previous day: craggy peaks ringing dozens of small lakes and creek-fed meadows. Below me I could see our campsite, the tent a cream-and-blue speck against the green of the alpine grasses. I saw Dad walk into view from behind a stand of trees, his figure so small that it was hard even to discern his legs and arms. My first instinct was to shout at him, to get his attention. *Look, Dad, see how high I climbed? See me, way up here? See me, married now, a grown-up? See me?*

It's a strange thing to look down on one's dad like that. Fathers aren't supposed to shrink. They're supposed to stay bigger than you forever. But size is relative. These days I lean over to hug my dad, yet I still feel like he's bigger than me. I still imagine the picture of him on South Sister, sitting above the clouds. I still feel his strong shoulders moving beneath my arms as he carries me up the trail. After seeing Dad from such a height, I began to clamber back toward our campsite. I paused whenever I caught a glimpse of the tent or Dad. Each grew bigger by the minute. At the bottom of the slope, I emerged from the trees, and there was everything in its place: Dad sitting with his back against a rock, watching the lake; our tent, swaying slightly in the breeze; a bright teal fleece draped over the branch of a pine tree.

"How was the hike?" asked Dad.

"Great," I said. "I could see forever."

Genetics

I never thought that Christine and I would find ourselves sitting in the office of a genetics counselor. But there we were, perched on our chairs across the table from a young woman who was giving us a crash course in genetic defects. We stared at page after page of laminated pictures of chromosomes. She wanted us to have as much information as possible so that we could "make the best decision" about Christine's pregnancy. She didn't know that we already had.

When Christine was eighteen weeks along, her doctor talked her into a triple-screen test, a blood test that looks for elevated levels of certain substances. Based on the mother's age, weight, ethnicity, and so on, the doctor is able to assign various risk levels for several birth defects or abnormalities, such as spina bifida or Down syndrome. We weren't sure if we wanted to have this test done, since all it provides are the statistical probabilities. The doctor, though, told us just to do it. "If you don't do it now, you'll lose your chance," she said. "Go ahead and do it. It's harmless."

Christine originally had a one in a thousand chance of giving birth to a baby with Down syndrome. The triple screen revealed that those odds were something like one in three hundred. Not very high odds, to be sure, but still frightening to us as first-time parents. Not only was there nothing to be done about it, but the test hadn't even given us a diagnosis. All we now knew was that our baby had an increased likelihood of Down syndrome. One in three hundred is still considered to be long enough odds that parents don't have to worry or prepare, though of course this didn't change the way we reacted. But our second ultrasound revealed a hardening of the upper right chamber of our baby's heart. This, combined with the triple screen, raised the odds of our baby being born with Down syndrome to one in a hundred, and off we were shipped to the hospital.

This sort of information is a heavy burden for parents—perhaps too heavy. A generation or two earlier, parents had no knowledge of the various odds surrounding their baby's prenatal development. Birth itself was the time of revelation. Babies develop in a continuous process, and we were being given a fuzzy snapshot of one point in that development. Would things change on their own? What course would nature take? Why had we consented to the triple screen, which seemed to have given us nothing but cause for worry and fear?

Next we did what anyone else would do: we googled Down syndrome. Christine and I sat in front of our computer, looking at a list of over forty-three million hits. We read medical facts, blogs written by parents of kids with Down syndrome, and opinion pieces written by advocacy groups. We tried to learn without freaking ourselves out too much. "Hmm, that's interesting— hearing loss and congenital heart disease are more common among children with Downs." "Oh, really? I didn't know that." Our voices were casual, but we weren't. We both knew that no amount of information could really prepare us.

Christine's cousin Katelyn was born with spinal muscular atrophy, a genetic defect that doesn't allow her muscles to develop sufficiently. Her type of SMA had only a small effect on her as a tiny baby, but as she grew, her parents noticed that she wasn't growing normally. She never rolled over, and she had to be helped into a sitting position. Soon it became clear that something was seriously wrong. There is no medical cure for SMA. Katelyn will never have enough strength to roll over in bed, walk, or eat food on her own. The prognosis for children with this form of SMA isn't good. It's possible that, at the age of seven, Katelyn has already lived much of her life.

With Katelyn's condition, daily life is hazardous. Catching a simple cold could be fatal, since she lacks the strength to cough up phlegm. Eating even tiny bites of a peanut butter and jelly sandwich could choke her. She can't turn on lights or open doors, and her diaphragm muscles are so weak that it's not easy to hear her if she calls for help. Life is a struggle, both for Katelyn and her family.

Life still has to be lived, though. It's impossible always to focus on the danger, or on the possible brevity of Katelyn's life. She still gets sent to her room for a time-out when she misbehaves. Ranch dressing licked from a friendly fingertip is a favorite treat. She loves to spin her motorized wheelchair, which she drives with deft touches of her right index finger. She zips all over the house, deck, and yard, trying to keep up with— and sometimes tow—two older sisters, as well as keep tabs on the motley collection of farm animals the girls raise.

Katelyn's parents expect her to be healed by God, a miracle for which they pray every day. They crave the prayers of their friends and family, believing that faith can move even medical mountains. They didn't know that Katelyn would be born with SMA. At the time of diagnosis, they weren't prepared for the countless challenges and obstacles they would confront each day. They didn't know they would one day sit beside their youngest daughter and hear her asking for oxygen and telling them that she didn't want to die. What they did know was that they loved Katelyn, and they wanted to see her thrive in whatever ways she was able. So they learned how to help their weak, helpless baby through the day, and then through the night. On it went, and on it goes.

I tried to picture myself caring for a baby with Down syndrome. I wondered if I would make some kind of peace with my child's condition. I asked myself if I could pray for healing, or whether I had too many questions and too much doubt. What was my baby doing right now in the womb? Was it developing properly? It was as if there were two babies growing inside of Christine, each existing in a kind of statistical limbo. One baby had Down syndrome, and the other didn't. Which one could Christine feel kicking? Which one would I meet in several months?

One night I was looking again at the website of the National Down Syndrome Society. At the top of the page is a small box that flashes portraits of children and adults with Down syndrome. Every few seconds a new picture pops up. One face arrested me. A baby boy, about six months old, is grinning at the camera. His chubby hands are clasped tightly together on his chest. He has dark blue eyes and short, fuzzy hair. He is utterly charming. My breath caught in my throat when

I saw him, but as quickly as he appeared, he was gone, replaced by the next picture. I sat frozen in front of the computer screen, waiting for the slide show to cycle back to him. There he was. I tried to memorize his face, my own face only inches from the screen.

I was terrified of having a son who is mentally or physically disabled. I feel helpless and awkward around someone with a disability. I experience a sense of dread when I encounter difference. I'd rather stay at home than go with my church to sing Christmas carols with the residents of Harbor House; I keep my headphones on when I'm studying at Starbucks and that retarded man drives his wheelchair through the door. How would I treat my own son?

My imagination needed to be given a new vision. Looking at that baby's grinning face, I could imagine myself looking at my own disabled child. This isn't something to be proud of: it's like bragging that I'm not *that* racist. But it was the first shoot sprouting from arid ground. I glimpsed who I might be, and who my child might be, and I realized that before things got too complicated, we could begin by smiling at each other. And somehow, that was enough for that moment. It was enough to carry me through meeting with the genetics counselor.

The office we were looking for was hard to find. We walked down the long hallway of the children's ward, the colorful murals on its walls at odds with the hushed conversations of the doctors and nurses we passed. We smelled a stomach-turning mixture of cafeteria food and cleaning products. Standing in the small elevator that would take us to the right floor, I could hear my heart beating in my ear. This is a routine appointment, I told myself, lots of parents have this. That didn't make me feel any better. I suddenly wondered, *Will our marriage survive the birth of a disabled baby or a miscarriage?*

So there we were, perched on our chairs. The counselor explained that the only way to be sure about our baby's condition would be to get an amniocentesis. The doctor would insert a long, thin needle through Christine's abdomen and into her uterus, taking a sample of the amniotic fluid. This would tell us conclusively whether the baby had Down syndrome, and if the result was positive, we could make a decision about terminating the pregnancy. Most parents choose to do the amniocentesis, and most parents who receive a positive result choose to abort.

I know that countless other families have gone through this same briefing. It's excruciating to hear that your baby may be abnormal, and I'm sure that no family makes their decision without agony. But for Christine and me, there wasn't really a decision to make, but only one to accept, though that didn't make it easy. We'd already seen our son stretching his legs during an ultrasound. We'd already heard his heart beating so very fast. We each had a keen sense that the life inside of Christine needed us to protect him. Inside the womb, he was safe, cared for intimately and completely by Christine's body, which was devoting much of its energy to his growth. The fetus inside Christine was dependent on her, and a possible genetic defect didn't change that. In either event, the dependence was total. And so, we figured, was our responsibility. We needed to let Christine's body do its work. And after birth, we needed to re-create, as far as we were able, the safety and security of the womb as the baby grew into its life.

An amniocentesis would tell us whether our baby had Down syndrome. It would also increase the risk of a miscarriage, and no further knowledge was going to change our decision to carry our baby to term. So we walked out of the office knowing what we knew when we walked in: that we'd meet our son in four or five months. There was no reason to frighten him with an unnecessary medical procedure. Christine and I were frightened enough for the three of us.

In the weeks following our visit to the genetics counselor, we worried a good deal. We told our parents and a few close friends about our increased chances of having a disabled child. We read more about Down syndrome. We prayed, or at least tried to. And I found myself beginning to cope. I couldn't spend every day worrying about my son's genetics. Christine and I looked at baby clothes together. I assembled the crib. We went out for coffee and talked about the weather and our next vacation. We carried on as if everything were okay. Which, regardless of the state of our son's chromosomes, it was.

Snow

Our basement home is warm and snug; lamplight spreads like butter across the snow outside. Christine nests on the couch beneath layers of fleece and down. I dry my hands at the kitchen sink. Clean mugs *drip drip drip* on the dish rack. Each counter and shelf is dusted and on its best behavior. Behind a closed door waits the nursery: crib sheets crisp, books shelved according to height, space heater humming in the dark. Soft animals wait to meet their new owner. The ceiling creaks, settles. Christine burrows deeper beneath her blankets. Snow falls. Baby shifts once, twice.

I walk to the nursery, open the door, and stand in the darkness. I close the door and walk to the bathroom; my reflection is without expression. The floor creaks as I walk back to the kitchen. I pour cold water into a glass that I lift from the drying rack. I take a sip and stare out the window.

Christine moves on the couch, soft grunts escaping her lips as she rolls over. I stand still in the kitchen, looking at the freshly cleaned floor. It is January 20th, one day before our due date. Everything is ready; everything is waiting. Snow falls through the shaft of light outside our window, turning gold before settling in the dark. I pour the rest of the water down the drain. My hands shake as I set the glass on the rack to dry.

We take a walk. Our feet move carefully through the snow. Behind us two sets of footprints disappear around the block; ahead is a smooth, white blanket. Houses sleep behind shuttered eyes. Christine takes deep breaths that cloud the dark air. Her round face hangs between her stocking cap and her rainbow scarf like a full moon. Across the expanse of her belly, her jacket strains to remain buttoned. We stop beneath a streetlight.

Christine shifts in place; her hands inside her jacket pockets are moving slowly across the protrusions of baby's bones. He moves, stretches, testing his strength. Snowflakes sift down through the cone of illumination; Christine's wool cap is nearly white.

"We don't go as fast anymore," I tell Christine.

She smiles at me and finishes the sentence. "It just takes longer with three of us."

"I don't think I can do this," I say. The sidewalk stretches ahead of us, fading into the umbra beyond the streetlight. A handful of snow drops from a branch beside us with the sound of falling sugar. I take deep breaths, the vapor rising through the falling snow. Christine takes my arm and we begin to walk. Slowly, through the new snow, we make it home again.

Birth

Christine's labor started out pleasantly enough at 2:00 AM, considering it involved enough pain to make her suck air and place a death grip on anything handy. We watched episode after episode of *The West Wing*, pausing the show whenever the pain was too intense. President Bartlett and his intrepid staff would freeze midsentence while Christine gasped; solving the nation's crises would have to wait for a few more minutes. During the contractions, Christine and I faced each other, our foreheads touching as we held hands. In between, I helped Christine nestle into her pillows, where she waited for the next wave of pain to break.

Ten hours later, at noon, things were worse. We'd moved from the couch in our house to the admitting room at the hospital. The well-worn copy of *Reader's Digest* that I found beside the hospital bed was proving useless—laughter was not the best medicine, and Christine wasn't interested in increasing her word power. That left me with no props, and I felt exposed and useless. I didn't know what to say or do. I wanted to stay right beside Christine as her strong rock, but I felt like running down the hall and locking myself in a supply closet until it was all over. So I settled for babbling about whatever came into my head, and whenever another contraction washed over Christine, we held hands until our knuckles turned white. As each wave of pain ebbed, I brushed her hair back from her damp forehead.

We were eventually admitted to our birthing room. Early in the afternoon, we decided that it would be best for Christine to have an epidural so she could rest for a few hours and dilate completely. I watched the doctor insert a long, flexible tube into Christine's spine, a section of the body that it's normally unwise to monkey with. Soon Christine reported that her pain was subsiding, as was her ability to feel or move her body below the waist. This trade-off seemed to be worth it, though. When her sister, Lisa, arrived, the three of us began to chat about crucial subjects like Lisa's drive and the weather. A semblance of normalcy settled over the room, though spikes of worry still poked through my defenses every few minutes.

A short while later, our fragile calm shattered. Christine was lying flat on her back, resting, and Lisa had stepped out of the room to make a phone call. Christine fainted, her head rolled to the side, and she vomited. Then she stopped breathing and her upper body began to shake and twitch. One of her machines began to beep. All of this happened quickly, like when a garden hose gets a kink in it and the water abruptly stops. For me, time slowed to a speed that was unlivable; how could I be watching my wife die just before our son was born?

Later we learned that this was all relatively routine. Because of the epidural, Christine's blood pressure was lower than usual. As she lay on her back, the baby's full weight pressed down on Christine's vena cava vein and cut off the flow of blood to her brain. A nurse was at her side in seconds. She reacted calmly and did some nursey things. She rolled Christine onto her side to restore the blood flow to her brain, wiped up the vomit, adjusted her IV tubes, and then propped her up on a bunch of pillows. One of the nursey things she should have done was to tell me that Christine would be fine. Either that or give me a heavy dose of sedatives.

Christine began to breathe again. She opened her eyes — so slowly, it seemed — and their brightness physically hurt me. I tried to smile. Christine was unaware of what had just happened. I held my mask of calm and confidence to my face, but I feared that the cracks in my voice would betray me. Not wanting to worry Christine, I asked Lisa to step into the room for a minute while I went to the restroom. I locked the door and collapsed against the wall, sliding slowly down into the corner. I bit on my fist and cried uncontrollably, my whole body shaking against the cold tiles.

When my defenses are down—late at night or when I'm lonely—I often consider why I collapsed, why I fled that hospital room. I think it comes down to my being scared. How was I scared? Let me count the ways: scared of pain; scared of becoming a parent; scared of my own shortcomings, and of discovering more; scared that Christine was going to die, and that I would lose my best friend; scared of becoming a single parent on the day of my son's birth; scared of hospitals. Such was my state, curled up and crying on the bathroom floor. Not a promising start to fatherhood.

Two things got me up. The first was the realization that I was sitting beside a toilet. I open doors with one finger and flush public toilets with my foot. If I had to keep crying, fine, but not while I was camped out in a germ factory. The second was the need to touch Christine. After I washed my hands thoroughly, of course.

It had been only minutes earlier that I'd thought she was dying. I'll deal with my feelings later, I told myself, but now I need to be with my wife. After cleaning myself up, I reentered the birthing room and sat down next to Christine. I held her hand. We spoke about delivery-room concerns—how her legs felt, how many centimeters dilated she was, when we thought the baby might be born. I told her I loved her. I put my hand on her stomach and felt our son squirming this way and that, seemingly all elbows and knees. Christine's skin looked almost transparent in the afternoon light. Blue veins traced urgent paths across her stomach. After a while, the baby seemed more restful. Perhaps he knew, on some level, what the contractions all around him meant. Perhaps he was gathering himself for what came next.

Sometimes I think that what happened to me that afternoon is just another example of a typical male trait. Something difficult happened, and rather than dealing with it and sharing it with my wife, I buried it and acted like nothing was wrong. I don't really believe that story, though. That kind of story is poisonous, leaching a steady trickle of toxins into the groundwater of my heart.

The story I believe is simpler and better. It's a story about the way life works. Getting my butt off that bathroom floor was a recognition that life — my life, Christine's life, the baby's life — was still happening. Time didn't stop when I slammed the bathroom door. Our baby was still being squished and pushed by his mother's uterus. Christine was still focusing on her body, trying to listen to its whispers and shouts. It was still nearly time for me to meet my son. That afternoon, some big words—fatherhood, responsibility, love—found me and reached out their hands. As they pulled me to my feet, they spoke to me. You'll be okay, they told me. Welcome to the club. You don't have to have the answers or understand everything. You just have to be available. You just have to do the next thing.

In the evening, our friends Aaron and Lauren came to visit. She was six months pregnant, so it was probably fortunate that they arrived when Christine was resting comfortably. While Lauren went to Christine's side and wiped her forehead with a cool washcloth, Aaron asked if anything needed doing, and we agreed that some crappy cafeteria food would be just the thing. We took part in the ordinary goodness of sharing a meal, except for Christine, who continued to enjoy her water and lollipops. We passed around the french fries until the styrofoam boxes were empty. Life kept happening, even under those altered conditions. The nurse checked the vital signs of Christine and the baby. Aaron and Lauren put on their coats, drawing out their goodbyes and adding extra blessings. Time ticked by. Christine and I watched some television. The nurse came again. We dozed. And around 5:00 AM, Christine gave birth to our healthy son, Nicholas, who turned out to be the ugliest, purplest, tiniest, most amazing person that I'd ever seen. I never did have time to go back and finish my cry on the bathroom floor; I was too busy learning how to swaddle my son, and calling my parents and my brother, and making sure the car seat was installed correctly, and a hundred other things that you do when you're a husband, a father, and a member of the tribe.

Interlude

Fish out of Water

You landed in a world of air,
a slick purple fish out of water
hooked to your mother
by a red cord of blood.
Before you could drown
in this place of noise and chrome
your mother pulled you into the boat
of her arms. Your round lips
mouthed the air, bubbling
the news of your being.
Your tiny twitches and flops broke
in waves across our hearts.
From the first moment you tugged
on our lives there was no question
of throwing you back.

Church

The first few weeks after Nicholas was born, I felt inordinately proud, at least when I was awake enough to notice. Much of the time I felt exhausted and overwhelmed as I struggled to balance being a dad with being a student, husband, and friend. Going out was exciting, though. Taking my new son out in public was a chance for me to show the world just how virile and strong I was, to demonstrate the stunning and irreplaceable contribution I'd made to the future of the human race. I was Mufasa at the beginning of *The Lion King*, standing atop Pride Rock with baby Simba, and everyone around us, though muted by awe, might break into song and dance at any time.

The first time we brought Nicholas to church, Christine carried him against her chest in a baby carrier. I locked the car and grabbed the diaper bag, turning toward Christine just in time to see Nicholas spit several ounces of milk out of his mouth, a common enough occurrence. Only this time, since he was nestled snugly against Christine, the stream of milk disappeared neatly down her cleavage. Gone, without a trace. Nicholas treated this as an unremarkable event, closing his eyes and laying his head down. Christine, I could tell, was on the edge between laughing and crying. Her eyebrows were raised, and the corners of her mouth were twitching up and down.

We evaluated the situation for its level of embarrassment—*Should we go home and change? Do we have time? Where's the rag?*—but as we stared down Christine's shirt, it was clear that the milk really had disappeared. Whether her undershirt had soaked it up or we'd witnessed an odd little miracle wasn't clear. One thing was clear, however: standing in front of the church and staring down Christine's cleavage was becoming awkward.

Even though newborns can't see more than a few feet, as we brought Nicholas through the front door, I was embarrassed. I saw our church with different eyes, and it suddenly seemed painfully hokey. I'm sure Nicholas wasn't accusing me of anything, but I felt guilty for bringing him to such a ragtag place. Didn't my son deserve the best? No imagination could stretch far enough to call this place the best. The stained-glass windows are an eyesore. In one, our Lord and Savior appears to have fallen asleep midconversation. A woman, flanked by several children, gazes up at his serene face, perhaps expecting another parable, but Jesus has had it, and he's closed his eyes. In another, Jesus' halo resembles a red-and-white life ring, ready to save novice swimmers at a nod from his head. The overhead projector wheezes, there are typos in the song lyrics, the guitar is out of sync with the drums, and children are crying. Welcome to church, Son.

We go downstairs for coffee as soon as the service ends. Our church rents space from a more established church, whose members regard us suspiciously as definitely too loud and possibly up to no good, so our pastor always herds us into the basement as quickly as possible. That morning we stepped carefully down the stairs, and the noise of conversation swelled and broke over our small family as we entered the room. Nicholas seemed too tiny for life in this particular world. What does he, with his stretches and grunts, have to do with small talk and Danishes?

But slowly we began to connect in conversation with small groups of people. Our pastor bounced over to tell us some horror stories about his own experience as a new parent—*Let me tell you, let me tell you, stumbling on the stairs at night while holding a tiny baby is something you'll never forget!* A friend told us that when he and his wife arrived home from the hospital with their daughter, they laid her on a blanket on the floor and stared at her for hours—*And she just stared right back!*

We sipped coffee. We told people Nicholas's birth weight and length again and again. A woman told us that her husband had been able, somehow, to sleep through the nighttime cries of all of their children—*He swore in the morning that he hadn't heard anything!* I was pulled aside by another dad and given the requisite speech—*You think you're tired now? Wait until you have four!*

This is our church, week in and week out. This is where we light candles during the dark of Advent. This is where we snack on stale tortilla chips in the basement after the service. This is where a woman with a cold drags her fingers underneath her nose before reaching for Nicholas's hand. This is where kids run, yelling and laughing, between our legs, while we chat with friends, and where a guy gives me the advice, *Get out of the house as much as you can. Your wife has to stay home, but you don't!* This is where we confess our failures and pray for each other, where we take communion and sign our names on a clipboard to bake cupcakes for the homeless. This is where people bring us dinner in Tupperware, where our son is passed from arm to admiring arm. This is our church, week in and week out.

The miracle of church is that familiarity breeds, not contempt, but comfort. It's not the artistry of the stained glass that pulls us back; it's the people. It's wanting Nicholas to be connected to something bigger than himself—bigger even than his family. At church we're part of a body that meets, week by week, to light a candle against the darkness of individualism. It's this body—this motley collection of broken and beautiful aunts and uncles and brothers and sisters—that teaches Nicholas that church is worth showing up for.

I love to wear Nicholas in a baby carrier when we go to church, though staying awake with a space heater strapped to my chest is nearly impossible. The pews are comfortable, and the light is ochre. As the sermon begins, I let my head nod down, savor the slight burn behind my eyelids, and give up the fight. I hear enough about God in graduate school nowadays. What I need is rest. What I need is to be in sync, breath by breath, with my sleeping son. What I need is to wake to the smell of freshly percolating church coffee, to the sound of Christine's sweet voice singing a hymn, to the sight of familiar faces lifted in song.

Seasons of Sleep

They say that you never know what you've got until it's gone, and I can only assume that they—whoever *they* are—are talking about sleep. They also say humans need sleep to survive, and I can only assume that young parents aren't considered human, since I'm almost positive that I didn't really sleep in the first months of Nicholas's life, which was not a good thing. The only upside was that I definitely would have survived a zombie attack, since the zombies would have assumed I was one of them already.

Twenty-eight years of blissful slumber came to a screeching halt on that cold January night Nicholas was born. The screeching came from two rooms down the hall in the hospital ward. Christine was resting in relative peace, still hours away from delivery. But a lady—I was pretty sure I was hearing a lady, or else a wild animal—was having her baby right then and yelling, "Ohhhhargh! It hurts, it hurts! *Oh ... my ... God!*" I huddled on the tiny couch beside my wife's bed, wondering what it would be like when my wife was yelling those same things. Christine looked over at me and asked, fearfully, "You don't think she has an epidural, do you?" I shook my head, eyes wide, and hoped I could get some sleep soon.

You see how slow on the uptake new dads are? I hoped I could get some sleep soon? From the present I can only smile and pat my past self on the head. When your wife is six centimeters dilated, you're not next in line to board the fast train to Sleepyville.

Nicholas was born in the early morning, and the first day of his life went by in a blur of weighings and swaddlings and excited conversations. Then night came—in Vancouver, in January, this seems to happen at about 3:30 PM—and I discovered one of the first commandments of fatherhood: thou shalt kiss sleep goodbye. That first night I got my best rest on a couch in the hospital hallway while holding my new son. My head flopped sideways at about a ninety degree angle, and I drooled all over my shoulder. When I woke up after what seemed like only twenty minutes—because it was only twenty minutes—both my legs were asleep, and when I tried to move them, Nicholas began to wake up. So instead of sleeping, I sat up awake, the pain in my neck and legs keeping me alert. Alert enough to understand the second commandment of fatherhood: baby's sleep is *always* more important than your own.

This experience isn't common to all new dads. A seasoned father I knew told me—sounding oddly proud, I thought—that'd he'd never gotten up in the middle of the night with any one of his three kids. From what I've observed, however, most new dads of my generation want to be more involved in the raising of their kids than their own dads were in raising them, so leaving mom on her own every night just isn't an option. And it's not like I had an important job to fall back on. I knew some dads who *had* to have sleep—*I can't be tired at work … the fate of the free world depends on my being well rested!*—but my job was dispensable, seeing as how I was studying art and theology full-time. (I did try it out one night. Me: "Honey, I'm going to sleep on the couch tonight and get eight hours. If I'm not fully rested tomorrow, who will answer the question in class about Niebuhr's impact on Christian political activism?" Christine: "Someone else?" Me: "Pass the burp cloth.")

My studies—and everything else in my life, really—became a blur, and only the moments I spent with Nicholas retained any sort of clarity. In between classes, I would stumble down to the library to catch a quick nap. There was no question of actually completing any work. What I needed was enough of a nap so I could stay awake through at least the first half of my next class before falling asleep again. I'd plop my head down on a book, drool into the binding, and wake with one minute to get to a class two flights of stairs above me. These were the days I was functioning well.

Nicholas, who slept as much as eighteen hours some days, was unable to coordinate that sleeping with our schedule. He'd happily sack out on the couch during the day with all the lights on. We'd bang dishes, vacuum, and make a general ruckus, and he'd continue to snore contentedly. Then, when 10:00 PM rolled around, Nicholas would wake all the way up for his nightly round of screaming. The screaming didn't seem to help him fall asleep, and neither did the way he would thrash his arms and kick his legs. It was more like a full-body workout than a presleep routine, so early on we settled on wrapping him tightly in swaddling blankets and trying to shush him over the noise of his screaming.

Our doctor told us that a baby in the womb hears a volume of sound that's similar to the volume of a vacuum cleaner. So when the baby is out in the real world, things can seem pretty quiet. If you want your kid to hear something, you have to create enough noise to make an impression. In those early months, I'd take our tiny, screaming egg roll into the family room so Christine could get some sleep. Then I'd lay down on the couch, turn on the Discovery Channel, and hold Nicholas on my chest. As he screamed, I'd thump his back and sing whatever song I could think of, from "Amazing Grace" to "U Can't Touch This." This usually did the trick, and Nicholas would drift off to sleep on my chest after a mere hour or so. In the meantime, I'd get to see great programming, like a special on Genghis Khan that I watched three nights in a row. Trying to read the closed captioning without my glasses was tricky, but I'm pretty sure Genghis liked chugging fermented horse milk, a drink that would have put Nicholas right to sleep, I bet.

As restful as those first few months of fatherhood were, there came a time when we decided that Nicholas was ready to join the club of people able to fall asleep on their own. What I didn't realize was that this meant committing ourselves to one of several opposing methodologies. Picking a sleep technique is no small choice—it can alienate you from friends and loved ones, like if Al Gore's son decided to become a coal miner.

In the interest of full disclosure, I'll tell you that we chose the cry-it-out approach, which makes us either responsible or cruel. I'm not interested in entering the trenches of the sleep war. Regardless of whether parents toss their kids in bed at the stroke of six and lock the door until morning or co-sleep with their child on a hemp mattress until the kid heads off to college, I've noticed that nearly all former kids know how to sleep. So we did what worked for us and tried not to worry too much about what other people were doing. This meant that we would make sure Nicholas was ready for bed—fed, burped, bathed, diapered, read to, prayed for, swaddled, and kissed—and then we'd lay him down and leave his room. Uncertain of what he was supposed to *do* in his bed once he was there, Nicholas would begin to scream while we listened. Actually, while *I* listened. On many nights like this, Christine would go somewhere—pottery class, soccer practice, a coffee shop—and I would stay at home on the couch, listening to the screams. It was better that way. As we like to say, I'm the heartless one.

Unhappy baby noises come in quite a few varieties, from your run-of-the-mill cry to your full-blown screaming bloody murder. Handily, these cries were easy to differentiate on our baby monitor. The receiving end of the monitor, perched above our computer desk, had three green lights on it. The more noise Nicholas was making, the more lights would shine. One light meant that things were just fine—he was grunting about something, but he'd calm down on his own. Two lights on meant that he was really crying, but he would almost always get quieter with no intervention.

When he was lighting up the whole monitor, though, that sure was something to listen to. It's easy to second-guess yourself when your child screams in bed every night; if I screamed every time I did something, I'm pretty sure I'd stop doing it. Those nights I'd sit there on the couch, listening to Nicholas's cries coming through the monitor, as well as through the wall, and I'd wonder what he was thinking or trying to say. His tone of voice usually led me to assume it was something like, "I hate you I hate this get me out of this place *ahhh!*"

Going into his room certainly didn't make things any better, so at least I didn't have to torture myself by imagining that Nicholas was crying out for Daddy's love. When we experimented with going into his room to calm him down, he only screamed more loudly. Entering his room essentially reset the countdown timer for his going to sleep eventually. No, what he really wanted was to be unbundled and brought back to where the action was. Lying still in bed when there was stuff to look at and play with was an indignity beyond his ability to bear.

And mine. Because I was the one enforcing the cry-until-you-sleep policy, I felt a huge burden of guilt and doubt. I never really considered changing our plan of teaching Nicholas how to fall asleep on his own. It was more a matter of wondering why the plan that I knew was right had to feel so lousy. I suppose that each night, as Nicholas cried himself to sleep, I could have kept a journal of my feelings, exploring the nuances of my emotional reactions. Or I could have emailed my close friends, creating a YaYa Brotherhood of support and encouragement. Instead I watched a lot of professional wrestling on TV.

Wrestling is actually the perfect thing to watch when your wife is gone and you have to listen to your baby crying. If I tried to watch anything more engaging—*CSI: Miami*, say—it always went badly. Either I would find myself missing the plot of the show because I couldn't hear what was going on, or, more disturbingly, I'd find myself wishing that Nicholas would be quiet so I could listen. Once, as I strained to hear a painfully ... slow ... speech ... by ... David ... Caruso, I hopped up to turn off the monitor. That was when I knew I'd never watch that sort of show again while listening to Nicholas. If I was teaching Nicholas a skill that was somewhat painful for him, the least I could do was suffer a bit myself. And what, really, is more painful than watching pro wrestling?

I'm writing this from a later vantage point, so I know the story has a happy ending. As bad as we felt when Nicholas was crying, we always knew that he'd learn how to sleep well, and we were right. Before too long, he learned how to be a champion sleeper, going right to sleep and staying down the whole night. In the morning, he would always wake up happy as a clam, cooing in his crib as sunbeams slanted through his window. We'd go into his room to get him up, and he would smile at us like we were his favorite people in the world (and maybe we were, but he smiled exactly the same way at his favorite red lamp and at the painting of a sailboat on our wall). I'd open his swaddling blanket, and his little arms would pop out and shoot up into the air in a luxurious, full-body stretch. "Ahh," he'd say, or, "Goo." "You slept the whole night," we'd tell him, and he'd smile again.

The other morning I remembered how things used to be as I was awakened early—just before 6:00 AM—by the sound of Nicholas calling from his room. "Get up now? Daddy? Get up now?" I open his door and see him already standing in his crib. "It's morning?" he asks, and I reluctantly agree that *technically* it's morning. Nicholas happily shouts, "Play cars!" and jumps up and down. I get him out of bed and carry him down the hall, reminding him to whisper since Mama is still asleep. "Wee-per wee-per wee-per," he repeats quietly to himself. As soon as I set Nicholas down in the family room, he hops over to where his cars and trucks are lined up at a little gas station, and he lifts out a fire engine with two hands. "Noise?" he asks. I remind him that the buttons don't work, but that he can make a noise for it with his mouth, and I demonstrate. He turns away, unimpressed. "Noise?" he asks again and pushes the engine's buttons over and over.

Christine and I decided early on that battery-powered toys were verboten. Against the tinny intrusiveness of beeping trucks and shouting action figures, we try to hold to a model of creative play powered by imagination—never mind the fact that Nicholas, like most boys his age, thinks that battery-powered toys are *way* cooler than regular toys. No sooner had we set forth this wise decree then we received a ton of new battery-powered toys—not ingenious wooden handicrafts lovingly carved in the Bavarian Alps, but a glut of double-A, double-loud, double-annoying plastic junk. You know the kind of toy I'm talking about—the tricked-out 4 × 4 that screams, "Racing action go!" in the voice of that monster-truck announcer. Sometimes, while Nicholas is sleeping, the battery fairy visits his toys and takes the batteries she finds to the nearest recycling center.

I'm glad that at least *this* morning's vehicle of choice is silent. As Nicholas drives one car after another through his service station, I thank God for the nation of Columbia and, specifically, its coffee plantations. The coffeemaker is making friendly noises as I settle onto a corner of the couch with my first steaming mug. Through the window, I can see the first glow of morning sunlight as the fog begins to disintegrate like cotton candy dropped in a puddle. It's early, there's no denying it, and I'll admit I'm tired. But not *that* tired. Not I-have-a-newborn tired. Nicholas knows how to sleep now, even if he doesn't know how to sleep in. I imagine him lying in bed until noon when he's a surly teenager and realize that I'll miss these early mornings together.

So when Nicholas asks me to sit on the floor with him and drive cars up and down his ramp, I agree, knowing that this won't last forever. But first, I tell him, I need to refill my coffee mug.

Sex on Thursdays

After Nicholas was born, I was talking to a friend on the phone. He mentioned that his wife had been going to a group called Mothers of Preschoolers, and at one recent meeting, a speaker told the mothers that they should be having sex more often.

I checked to see if I'd heard that right. I had.

He said the speaker had recommended that the couples consider scheduling a "sex night" each week. That way, the husband would be sure of having regular sex, and the wife wouldn't have to wonder when her man would be bugging her for sex. "We've tried it, and it's great!" reported my friend. "I told my wife that she should feel free to go to MOPS whenever she wants!"

It's a mark of how much I've changed over the years that my friend's story sounded like a good idea to me, too. An obedient Christian boy, I'd waited until marriage to get past second base. I assumed that once I got married, everything would be perfect, and I'd have satisfying sex whenever I wanted. How have I gotten from there to considering the idea of sex night?

As newlyweds, the only limitations on our sex life were self-created. We were two kids fresh out of college with the time, energy, and privacy to enjoy our love. While I quickly learned that sex wasn't the effortless perfection I'd assumed it would be, Christine and I still enjoyed each other tremendously. There were, of course, times of sickness or busyness during which our intimacy suffered, but during the next five years of marriage we were, on the whole, happy. Neither one of us, however, was prepared for the changes that having a baby would bring. Intellectually, I understood that things would be different, but I didn't know just *how* different.

After Nicholas was born, Christine and I didn't have sex at all. At first that wasn't much of a hardship for me. I was still in graduate school, trying to manage course work along with the demands of a new baby, all the while getting a restful five hours of sleep a night. I barely had the wherewithal to eat and change my clothes occasionally, so summoning the physical and emotional energy for sex was out of the question. Not to mention that when you wear one stained sweatshirt all week, your sex appeal tends to take a nosedive.

If I was tired, Christine was exhausted. She wasn't able to sleep for more than an hour or two at a time, and she was constantly caring for Nicholas. More important, the physical reality of Christine's healing body meant that sex wasn't an option. When your wife pushes an eight-pound baby out of her vagina, there are bound to be consequences. For Christine, those consequences included stitches, pain, lowered mobility, and a gradual return to physical health.

For me, the consequences included a new relationship with my wife's body. Before Nicholas was born, I wasn't sure if I'd be able to cut the umbilical cord, even though I knew it was one of those daddy jobs I'd be expected to do. But when the time came, and the doctor handed me a deadly-looking pair of scissors, cutting the cord was a cinch. Two snips—like cutting through a piece of thin rope—and the job was done. It was easy because my senses were overwhelmed by what was happening just a few feet away. I was reasonably sure a tiny, wrinkled human had just squeezed out between Christine's legs, and there was blood everywhere, along with some other fluids I didn't recognize. By the time the doctor got Christine stitched up, cleaned up, and propped up, I knew I would never relate to my wife the same way again.

Further evidence of this change appeared in my bizarre reaction to Christine's hospital underwear. After she gave birth, Christine was given a pair of gauzy, hospital-issue undies, since that was the best way to hold in place absorbent pads that were soaking up a steady flow of blood. There was my soccer-playing, no-nonsense wife, decked out in a pair of see-through underwear. Pre-Nicholas, of course, I found sheer underwear attractive, but here I was thinking that *this* pair was attractive, too.

I realize that it's weird and possibly sick that I was attracted to my wife's institutional underwear just after she gave birth. But having a kid flipped a switch inside of me. It wasn't just that something new had been added to my normal life; everything in my normal life looked different.

It wasn't Christine's underwear at all, really; it was *Christine*. When I understood the bloody reality of grace—that my wife was giving her own life to our son—my love for Christine took on a new dimension. I still found her beautiful—attractive sexually and at so many other levels—but I also found beauty in the dark circles under her tired eyes, the sweat on her forehead, and the strength of her mother's body. And yes, even while she wore her hospital underwear, I was more attracted to Christine than I ever had been before.

Home from the hospital, Christine and I began learning how to live with another person. This wasn't an easy adjustment. Nicholas monopolized Christine's attention, her energy, and, most important, her body. Newborns eat every hour or two, all day and all night.

Since Nicholas was breast-feeding, there were few times that Nicholas wasn't in Christine's arms as both of them learned the steps of this new dance.

Unfortunately for Christine, this was a difficult dance. I'm sure there's a medical term for what Christine was suffering, but it seemed to me like a textbook case of nipple hickeys. I could hold Nicholas, sure, but every hour or two it was back to mom for another meal, and each time Nicholas latched on, Christine winced in pain. All I could do was watch, feeling useless and longing to help.

Christine was ready for me to help, too, but first her milk had to come in. One morning Christine stepped into the shower looking like herself, and a short while later—voila!—the curtain was flung open to reveal that my wife had been given a boob job by Mother Nature. There was no time, however, for shock and awe. Milk was rapidly dripping out of Christine's breasts onto the bathroom floor, and they hurt her so badly that she couldn't even dry them off. It took about five seconds for me to learn an important lesson: no matter how good she looked, Christine's new figure was for Nicholas and Nicholas only. Sounding like an ER doctor, Christine started issuing commands: "Gimme three burp cloths, two pillows, and a hungry baby—stat!"

If I was surprised, Nicholas was blown away. Last time he checked, his food came out nice and slowly.

Now he was suddenly confronted with milk shooting fire-hose style from something larger than his head. He could hardly keep up. If he pulled away from Christine's nipple for even a second to catch his breath, a jet of milk would blast his face and cover his downy eyebrows with froth. There was nothing for it but to plunge back in, like a drowning man trying to drink his way out of a swimming pool.

At first I was fine with our breast-feeding arrangement. Each thing that baby Nicholas did was fascinating, since I'd never watched a baby do so much as blink. I observed him wrinkle his eyebrows while he slept; I was riveted when his red lips latched on to Christine's breast. But then it dawned on me: we're playing a zero-sum game here. Nicholas enjoys intimacy with Christine, and, therefore, I don't. There's no such thing as baby and dad sharing mom's body. I was watching from the bench, longing to get back in the game—and feeling guilty for even thinking that.

As the weeks went by, though, *some* things began to change for the better on their own. Christine's body learned how much milk was needed to keep up with the appetite of our growing boy, and her breasts no longer ached. She began pumping, filling bottles drop by precious drop with milk, and the *errERRerrERR* of her pump became one more familiar voice in our increasingly noisy household. Armed with a bottle of breast-milk, I sat on the couch and fed my son for the first time. After a false start, during which Nicholas tried to latch on to my sweatshirt, it went just fine. Nicholas lay warm in my lap, sucking his milk and making the cutest little grunts I'd ever heard. There is something primal about the way a baby eats, and by sharing that ritual, Nicholas and I were bound more closely together. And I discovered that Christine and I were drawn together, too, by caring for our new son.

Not everything automatically changed for the better, though. Christine and I found that it was easy—frighteningly easy—to let the busyness of our new life as parents interfere with our relationship. It's a truism these days that everyone's busy, but new parents are especially busy and so, so tired. In the mornings, one of us is up early with Nicholas while the other gets a few extra minutes of sleep. When the sun rises, we're buying groceries, writing, going to Kindermusik, playing blocks with Nicholas, and doing the thousand other little things that make a household function. Nights, I'm learning barre chords at guitar class, or Christine is whipping up a dessert in cooking class, or we're folding laundry and watching *The Colbert Report*—and jumping up during the ads to check on that eBay bid.

Just because Christine's body is back to normal and we're adjusting to our new schedule as parents doesn't mean that our relationship looks like it did before Nicholas was born. Our marriage seems to have seasons, each of which brings its own particular pleasures. One season leads inexorably to the next; there's no going back. Before I was married, and before I had Nicholas, sex night would have sounded odd. Maybe even wrong. You can't program a relationship like that, can you? Intimacy shouldn't be scheduled like any other appointment, should it?

I'm growing increasingly fond of the saying "Don't should all over yourself." My life as a father and a husband confirms the truth of this nearly every day. I can't live my life in the clouds of shoulds and oughts. Life happens on the ground; we live it where we are, not where we think we should be. When Christine and I were first married, we were more adventurous. Not that we did anything too weird, mind you, but there *was* that one afternoon on the futon with the body paint. Now? If we tried that, I bet Nicholas would probably wake up early from his nap, not to mention we'd need to do an extra load of laundry to clean the futon cover. That was then, and this is now. Sometimes having Nicholas around can actually spice up our sex life, like on those rare mornings when we wake up with the sun shining in our bedroom window—Nicholas is *still* sleeping?—and starting anything romantic feels risky. Risky, but fun!

But for us—for any parent—mornings like that are the exceptions to the rule. Most mornings, nothing more thrilling happens than waking up early to read Richard Scarry books with Nicholas, and most nights we're too tired to do much more than read *Harry Potter* beside each other in bed and fall asleep spooning. We're busy, sure, and tired, but we're busy and tired together. This is our now, and it's good.

Sometimes there is a moment just after Christine and I make love. We rest in the warmth of each other's arms. Quiet covers us like a blanket. Before I breathe in, I open my eyes, and time stretches long in the silence. Then, in the darkness, carefully, I take my first breath. My chest expands, our embrace tightens, and the two of us choose again to make the journey together. And thanks to MOPS and our appointment calendar, we stand a good chance of experiencing this moment every week on Thursday nights.

Soft Spot

When Nicholas is ready to sleep, his already tenuous grip on his motor skills loosens and he becomes a sort of baby stuntman. He'll try things that are ridiculously beyond his nine-month-old abilities, like leaping from one side of his playpen to the other, or simultaneously biting the ivy plant and pulling books off the shelf. Or he'll try walking from the couch to the armchair, which would be easy, if only he could walk. Invariably, he ends up stuck in an awkward position, trapped like a turtle on its back. We encourage him—*You'll be able to do that in a few months, honey*—pick him up, and pack him off to bed.

Nicholas and I have a bedtime ritual. I carry him into his room, and we sit in the rocking chair to read a story together. Lately it's been *That's Not My Dinosaur!* by Fiona Watt. Christine gets bored with these baby books—*Okay, already, I freakin' know it's not your dinosaur!*—and changes the words when she reads. I can see why she does this, since most days she spends her time talking to a person with a five-word vocabulary. For me, though, there's something appealing, after a day spent studying theology, about simple plots and clear resolutions.

The protagonist, a white mouse, doesn't know much, but he knows which dinosaur is his and which ones aren't. "That's not my dinosaur," he reports. "Its body is too squashy." He marches right past the dinosaurs that aren't his—too fuzzy, too slippery, too rough. Nicholas reaches his fingers out on each page, feeling for just the right spot to confirm the mouse's judgment: tail, flippers, horns. We reach the last page together, each time the first time. "That's my dinosaur! Its spines are so soft." And it's true; they are. Nicholas brushes the purple fuzz that crowns this dinosaur's spine, petting it again and again. I feel it, too; it feels good. Good to be sure of something. Good to know who is whose.

But things change. Nicholas's memory is more like a sieve than a steel trap. Before long, he turns the last page, hiding the dinosaur with the so-soft spines in the book once again. Then there's nothing for it but to flip to the front and start again. Is this my dinosaur? We'll keep looking, he and I, until we find it; we'll look as long as it takes.

I know we're done when Nicholas stops turning the pages. We have to leave our mouse in midsearch, looking and looking until we open the book again. I settle Nicholas across my lap, his head in the crook of my left arm, turn out the light, and give him his bottle. He now has plenty to do for the next ten minutes: drinking, holding his bottle jauntily with just one hand, looking around the dark room, and trying to yank off my glasses. It's me who gets bored.

That's why I felt so guilty when I heard about a mother who prays for her baby as he nurses. You feed your baby every day, she said, so it's perfect. Besides, what else are you doing during that time? She makes a good point: I'm doing nothing. What I'd like to be doing—watching a ball game with headphones on, for example—isn't feasible. So of course I feel guilty, thinking of all that wasted prayer time, all those missed chances. How different would my son's life be if I pray every time I give him a bottle at night? When he's a crazed hermit prospecting in the Yukon at age forty, will I have my lack of bedtime prayer to blame?

So I determine to pray. This is what model parents do, I tell myself, and I've always wanted to be a model. When Nicholas starts to suck, I start to pray. It goes something like this:

God, thank you for this time with Nicholas. Thank you so much for him. He's so beautiful and small. He can hardly do a thing for himself. Today he was sitting up and trying to get a toy that was two feet in front of him. He leaned so far forward that he fell over and landed on his face. It didn't hurt, luckily, but it sure made him mad. As if someone else had done it to him! Well, he isn't the brightest bulb in the chandelier, that's for sure. Ah, what a kid!

My thoughts snap back. Aren't I supposed to be praying? I take a deep breath, close my eyes, and continue.

Anyway, God, thanks for Nicholas. I want so much for him as he grows. Please keep him healthy and strong. What would we do if he was ill or injured? The thought makes me sick. I can't imagine him with wires hooked up to his smooth little chest, with tubes down his nostrils. He wouldn't understand what was happening. He'd be so scared. Hospitals are like that. How have I escaped them for so long? Does that mean that I've got it coming? Or that he does? Is this what it's like to be a parent? God, it's scary! Oh, right. God. So, God, thanks for this time here in the dark with Nicholas. It's so good to know that you're listening. So good to know you love us. So good . . .

I wake with a jerk. Nicholas is looking at me. His bottle is dry, but he's still sucking, making faint hissing noises. I've been asleep for a quarter of an hour, which doesn't seem to have bothered him. I lift him onto my chest before standing up from the rocker. In one of his rare displays of tenderness, he puts his head against my chest, and I bow my head to kiss him. My lips find his hair, warm and soft and fine. I press down, willing him to feel some of what I feel. Startlingly, as my lips press down, they find the soft spot—the anterior fontanel— between his growing skull bones. My kiss seems to penetrate his head. There's something alien about this, something invasive; I'm where I don't belong. Kisses connect from the outside, and this one feels like I'm on the inside. I wonder if I'm pressing on his brain, and if it hurts.

Free of these worries and obsessively curious, Nicholas spins his head to look around the room, and I feel the harder sections of his skull moving beneath my lips. I pull my lips back, and we stand up, the rocking chair swinging back from us to *knock knock* the wall. We stand in the center of his room and spin slowly, say-ing goodnight as we go. "Goodnight changing table. Goodnight books. Goodnight lion." We reach his crib. "Goodnight baby." I feel fingers exploring my face, my nose, then rubbing against my stubble. *That's my dad. His face is so rough.* I lay Nicholas down in his crib, mak-ing a more reasonable attempt at prayer: "Sleep well, little one." As he rolls over to snuggle with his blanket, I slide my middle finger up his forehead and into his hair, gently touching his fontanel. I know that his growing skull will soon close that soft spot. Soon his head will be hard enough to smash a soccer ball into a net. Soon enough, but not just yet. That's my baby. His head is so soft.

Generations

When Christine and I were married on May 27, 2000, my grandpa Nicholas couldn't attend the ceremony because of his failing health. In his place, he sent a poem, one of hundreds that he wrote for friends and family throughout his life. As we stood beneath arching oak trees in the dappled sunlight, his daughter Eloise read the poem to us. It recalled the joy of Grandpa's lifelong marriage and ended with these words:

> Let Corinthians thirteen
> Fill your hearts with shining gleam!
> David and his sweet Christine:
> Here's my love and deep esteem.

That wasn't the first time that Grandpa had spoken to me about First Corinthians thirteen. Several months before the wedding, while I was living with my parents in Santa Barbara, Grandpa came for a visit. The night before he left, I was folding clothes in the laundry room when Grandpa shuffled in wearing his plaid bathrobe. His wispy white hair and forehead shone in the overhead lights, and his slippers scuffed on the linoleum floor.

"Well, goodnight," he said. His voice was mellow, the deepest part of a clear stream.

I hugged him and felt his patchy whiskers scratch my neck. He put his hand on my arm and smiled. "You've been a good grandson. Keep following the way," he said as he leaned forward, near the point of tipping, "and keep taking care of Christine. Remember to read Corinthians thirteen when things get rough."

His hands sketched two shapes in the air between us. "Lives are different." His hands joined, fingers nesting. "But the differences we see in this life are only a preview of heaven. It would get pretty monotonous if you two always thought the same."

He lifted a basket from the floor and worked a while sorting socks. With his eyes on his job, he rocked back and forth before regaining his balance. "Well, you must not want to hear me lecture."

"Grandpa, I love to hear you talk," I said, almost pleading. I saw his eyes again, bright with a lifetime of good humor and love. We talked a bit more, folded a few more clothes, and said goodnight. As Grandpa turned to leave, he said, "I'll see you again, Lord willing."

Rookie Dad

In October, four months into my new marriage, I was sleeping at home in Santa Barbara. When the phone jarred us out of sleep before 5:00 AM, I knew what was coming. Christine answered with a worried voice. In my head I repeated the word *no* like a mantra, trying to hold off the avalanche of pain that was rushing toward me. Christine hung up and touched a warm hand to my shoulder. She paused. "That was your mom." Several hours later, after we'd had time to pull ourselves together—which really meant trying to get dressed and eat breakfast in between the tears—Christine and I went to my parents' home. I held tightly to my mom, thinking how tiny she felt in my arms.

Several days later our family gathered in Quarryville, Pennsylvania, for the funeral of Robert E. Nicholas. I remember a stream of people tearfully telling me what I already knew: my grandfather was a wonderful, loving man, and he had finally gone home to be with God. Soon it was time for the family viewing. I hung back, never having seen a dead body before, and watched other relatives enter the viewing room. I trusted their experience and judgment: if they wanted to see him, then maybe I should, too. As I eased into the room, the hair on my neck stood up. I finally peeked into the open casket, and I found myself looking at a wax likeness, an image. This wasn't Grandpa. Grandpa puttered around his apartment, watched the Weather Channel, banged on his manual typewriter, and snored in his recliner. This representation wasn't close enough to give comfort, but it was close enough to hurt. I shuddered and walked quickly out into the sunlight, my throat aching with grief.

After Grandpa died, I began to miss his physical presence. I remembered the back rubs he used to give me when I was in grade school: he prayed me to sleep while his warm, rough hands moved in time with his words, up and down, back and forth. I thought of his body while he preached, rising up on his toes as he emphasized a point or told a punch line, his voice, like a cello, working the rich midregister. When he told stories at the dinner table, he'd interlock his fingers, elbows on the table, and as he moved left and right, leaning into the story, the heels of his palms would rub together. His legs bounced along with the beat of his conversation.

Two days after Grandpa's funeral in Pennsylvania, my aunt Bethann showed me his leather walking shoes, which he'd gotten as a gift. He hadn't used them much, partly because the pain in his legs and back limited his walking, and partly because he preferred his old shoes, imitation leather fastened with velcro. These new shoes were simply too nice to use. "You can have them if they fit you," said my aunt. I leaned forward to lace the shoes, feeling like I was trespassing. But as I tightened the laces and felt how the shoes supported my feet, I sensed that I'd found a link to Grandpa, a physical reminder of him.

At each family wedding since then, I've worn these shoes—and even tried to dance. It's important to me to let my memories of Grandpa walk into the present, beside me, as our family grows and changes. Recently, on a sunny Sunday morning in Southern California, I was wearing Grandpa's shoes when Nicholas was baptized.

When I was three months old, my grandpa, the Reverend Robert E. Nicholas, dipped his fingers into a simple silver chalice and sprinkled water on my forehead, baptizing me into the family of God. Now, twenty-eight years later, I am standing with my wife, my son, and my father in the front of the church. Dad's calloused fingers curl around that same chalice as he stands beside me; my hand rests on Christine's shoulder. *Love*, I think, *is patient. Love is kind.*

The pastor stands in front of my dad. He dips his fingers into the water and lifts them toward Nicholas, who is bouncing gently in Christine's arms. I watch Nicholas turn his attention toward this new thing, smiling. We hear the pastor's voice ring out, saying, "The Lord says, 'I will establish my covenant between me and thee and thy children after thee throughout their generations for an everlasting covenant, to be a God unto thee and to thy children after thee.'" Water rolls down Nicholas's face and he blinks in surprise.

The pastor takes Nicholas and holds him in front of his new family. I watch my son stare into row after row of smiles. *Love rejoices with the truth.* As the pastor prays, he blesses Nicholas by name, the name he shares with his great-grandfather. My right arm is around Christine's waist, my eyes on my son. *Love always protects, always trusts, always hopes, always perseveres.*

I can't take my eyes off Nicholas. Drops of water trace wet paths through his hair. My left hand feels the wiry strength of my father's shoulder. The pastor finishes his prayer and returns Nicholas to Christine's waiting arms. I lean toward my son and meet his eyes. It is the three of us; it is all of us. I understand that the past can touch the future. I look down. *Love never fails.*

Distance

One morning I woke up lonely. The responsibilities of fatherhood were crowding out everything that used to make me feel like a healthy human. In those rosy years BC—before children—I enjoyed a lot of casual friendships and activities, from playing ultimate frisbee to hanging with friends to writing poetry. I even had a best friend, Sam, after years of flying solo. Only weeks into being a new dad, though, life was darkening. At home, I felt like I should focus entirely on mother and baby. It seemed like I was constantly rocking Nicholas, or feeding him, or talking about sleep cycles and spit-up. My clothes were dirty, and I didn't shave. Things piled up. Outside the home, I could be found struggling to stay awake at school or waiting in line at the market to buy diapers, nursing pads, and hand sanitizer. Whatever social life I used to enjoy was dying, slowly and surely. And in the midst of this, I was very, *very* tired.

In the equation of my life, lonely plus tired equals depressed. I may have been a new dad, but at least I knew that my plummeting emotions would not be a good thing for our young family. We needed each other to be healthy and content. Nicholas had no problems in that respect. He was usually happy and putting on so much weight that I wondered if he was drinking polar bear milk. Christine seemed okay, too, even though she was tired and occasionally moody. She had a good support network and was getting to do what she'd always wanted: to stay at home with her first baby. (I can't resist mentioning that Canada provides fifty weeks of paid maternity leave. Yes, you read the words *fifty* and *paid* correctly, and yes, we're sneaking back across the border if we're ever ready to have another kid.)

Part of what I was feeling just comes with the territory. But during a rare moment in which I was able to think clearly—probably after several hours of sleep and four cups of coffee—I had a moment of mathematical revelation. I can't help being tired, I reasoned, so that means I need to change the other addend—loneliness—if I want to change the sum. Revelations don't usually come with detailed instructions for follow-up, though. Sure, I could put on a clean shirt and shave, but then what? How could I remake all those casual, but essential, friendships when I had so little time or energy? And more important, how should I go about having a best friend in another country when I could barely leave my home?

Getting back into casual friendships didn't turn out to be so hard, once I got over the hurdle of accepting my new position in life as a father. When I got married, I went through a period of mourning for my single life. I pouted about all the freedoms that I'd lost. And then I realized that trading the freedom to play video games all night for the freedom to love and be loved wasn't exactly a bad trade. My new life as a married man was better than my life as a single man. The same is true with my new life as a father. I'd lost the freedom to play ultimate frisbee on Saturday mornings, sure, but c'mon, I'd gained a baby! I knew that Nicholas was beyond awesome, and I knew I'd love him for life.

So I went back to my writing group, but this time as a different person. Being up with Nicholas the night before meant that I didn't have time to read Ruth's strong poem about her grandmother's hands as thoroughly as it deserved, and I had to leave the group after only forty-five minutes so I could catch the last bus home in time for Nicholas's dinner. But still, I was there. I was still regaining a bit of a life. Or, it would be better to say, I was learning how to live my new life.

My new life involved a lot more interruptions. I learned how to write email messages with Nicholas on my lap contributing his own important thoughts—

messages like *Dear Rick, How arebn mn nnnmbbbb.* I learned how to make phone calls that bore scant resemblance to human conversation: *Hey Mom! How are you? What? Can you say that again? Sorry, Nicholas was crying. Yeah, I'm fine. What? Hold on, Nicholas is fussy—I'm going to switch positions. Okay, I'm back. So anyway—eww!—sorry again, Nicholas just urped all over my leg. Hang on, I have to get a towel.* Despite the interruptions, though, I began to feel like part of the wider world again. I began to feel almost human. The only thing missing was Sam.

In my life, best friends don't grow on trees. As a teenager, I played basketball and Dungeons & Dragons with my buddies, but I didn't have a best friend. One day in a chapel service at my Christian high school, the speaker told the Old Testament story of David and Jonathan. I closed my eyes and leaned my head forward into my cupped hands—*the* prayer position to show how serious you were—and prayed that God would give me a friend like Jonathan.

I guess God wasn't in a rush, though, because I sped through the next year of high school and the four years of college after that without ever being one in spirit with anyone. Life kept happening. I got married. College friends moved out of town. I met new people and worked at new jobs. I bought toys, watched TV, surfed a lot, and went to church on Sundays. And I got used to living without a best friend. I stayed so busy that I usually forgot that I was lonely.

And then I met Sam. He and his wife, Jamie, moved to Austria to teach at the same time Christine and I did. Sam and I did everything together, and before you could say "Sprechen Sie Englisch?" we were fast friends. Having a best friend snuck up on me, maybe because it felt so normal. I found it hard to imagine what life was like before I met Sam; being together felt like the most natural thing in the world. I think guys are built to thrive when they have a best friend, like a fish in clear water. With Sam, I always feel more like the person I want to be—more like the person I was made to be.

After a long day of teaching in Vienna, we'd take the subway downtown together to the Schwedenplatz U-Bahn station. As darkness fell and the city lit up, we'd peel off our winter gloves just long enough to gulp down a piping hot kebab from the street vendors while we talked about our lives. We made each other sharper, and the feeling of being known and loved was the feeling of home. What I didn't know, though, was what would happen when we moved to Vancouver and Sam and Jamie stayed behind in Vienna. I knew I still needed Sam, but I feared that our friendship would wither like a grape pulled from the vine once we were separated by an ocean and two continents.

Distance

In *The Island of the Day Before*, Umberto Eco writes that "absence is to love as wind to fire: it extinguishes the little flame, it fans the big." That's all well and good, but it doesn't do squat for the fact that living thousands of miles away from your best friend sucks. But Christine and I had decided to move, despite what it did to our friendships. So Sam and I tried to make the best of things. We learned to email and to talk on the phone despite a nine-hour time difference. We did what we had to, but we didn't have to like it. Email and phone calls are no substitute for presence; friendships are made to be flesh and blood.

We learned to live, however unwillingly, with physical distance, but I wasn't prepared for the fact that becoming a dad would increase the distance between us yet again. I was exhausted, busy, stressed, emotional, lonely, and frequently covered in spit-up; how could I maintain my friendship with Sam? How could something that seemed so vital—to my sense of self, to my well-being, to the health of my wife and new son—seem so impossible?

I think Eco is right. Distance, while painful, is a kick in the pants, too. It's a call to decision. The harder it gets to hold on to a relationship, the more forcefully you have to commit yourself. It didn't escape my notice that this decision—that I was going to hang on to my friendship with Sam come hell or high water—might have some bearing on raising Nicholas. I've heard it said that the best thing a dad can do for his child is to love the child's mother deeply and faithfully. After all, kids notice a lot and draw their own conclusions. If that's true, then maybe the second-best thing a dad can do is have a lifelong best friend, someone he never stops loving no matter the distance.

The great thing about distance is that it can change. And guess what? Sam and Jamie had the good sense to get pregnant soon after Nicholas was born. Now we were locked in: in a few short years when our kids got married, we'd see each other all the time! Once little Eliza was born, we decided to fly to Michigan, where Sam and Jamie were now living, to finalize the betrothal. Maintaining friendships in the fog of fatherhood can seem monotonous—you can't help but long for a glimpse of the sun. When we finally found ourselves standing in Sam and Jamie's kitchen, erasing time and distance with our hugs and laughter, the light was so bright that it hurt my eyes.

Sometimes grace tackles blessing in a happy tangle of arms and legs. It turned out that our other friends from Austria, Steve and Linda, were able to travel to Michigan at the same time. Our families lived in the sunshine of each other's company, the days a blur of laughter and conversation. Our kids played together and made each other cry while we fixed bagel sandwiches and drank soda from Dixie cups. We rejoiced simply to be with each other, bodily, in the warmth of real presence.

I carry one memory from that trip in my pocket; it is smooth from being handled time and again. The sun has set and our kickball game has reached a raucous, grass-stained end. Nicholas is sleeping upstairs after partying to the point of exhaustion. Sam and Steve are sitting on patio chairs in the humid evening air, and I wander over with three beers and slouch down beside them. Our wives are inside the screened porch, and their laughter and light spills out across the yard. Across the dark lawn fireflies flare green. Our talk moves easily, naturally, a leaf riding the currents of a stream. A small girl traipsing through the grass pauses to look at us and ask, "What are you guys waiting for?"

Such a wonderful question. Surely we're waiting for *something*, right, like dessert or the start of the next game? Why else would we be sitting here? Steve chuckles. "We're not *waiting* for anything." He stops to smile and look at Sam and me. "This is it."

This *is* it, isn't it? This *is* what we're waiting for, after the pizza box is full of crusts, after the kickball sits forgotten on the grass and the table is covered with snapshots. This is what we're waiting for, after living in different countries, after the time spent flying and driving, the time spent feeling the ache of absent friends. We are waiting for this exact moment when we can sit in patio chairs and talk as the summer breathes its heat into the darkness.

I understand that this is what I've been waiting for every minute of my life. This is what I wanted that day I held my head in my hands and prayed for a best friend, because what I was really praying for was to be more fully human, more fully alive. My chest swells with love for my friends, my wife, my baby sleeping in the dark. This is what I crave for you, Son, this certainty of being loved and known. This is worth waiting for. Three friends, three chairs, and the hum of a summer night.

Have Baby, Will Travel

For some reason—possibly we were suffering from sleep deprivation when we made the decision—we are getting on an airplane with our baby today. When traveling with a baby, the entire day is a potential disaster, and not just the six hours that you're actually in the air. Now that it's the day of the trip—day in the technical sense of the clock saying AM—it feels like disaster is imminent. The alarm stabs its way into my consciousness, and I'm dimly aware that the sun won't rise for hours yet. Any coffee I drink now means more bathroom trips later—a luxury I can't afford—so I stumble around the dark house, banging into furniture and repeating the day's mantra: *please let baby be good, please let baby be good*.

Soon the car is packed, the engine is running, and we can't put off any longer that cruelest of parental duties: snatching our soundly sleeping son out of his cozy bed in the middle of the night. It kills us to think of how many hours we've spent trying to get him to stay *in* bed, but here we are yanking traveling clothes over his crying face. We almost hope he has some over-the-top illness—maybe a wet, hacking cough coupled with a shocking red rash from head to tiny toe—because then we could cancel our tickets!

Sadly, Nicholas is a paragon of health, so off we drive to the airport. We stayed up late packing and checked in online last night, which now means absolutely nothing, since we *still* have to wait in the same interminable line as everyone else to check our bags. The employee at the counter asks us for Nicholas's birth certificate just in case we grabbed someone else's child at 4:00 AM for a fun day of travel. One suitcase is overweight, and the other is under, so we crouch on the dirty tile floor and paw madly through our bags looking for heavy objects like a St. Bernard searching for survivors after an avalanche.

Once past check-in, we plod through the security line while trying to convince Nicholas that it will be *fun!* and *good!* to take away all his comfort items—blanket, stroller, snack, teddy, and yes, even his milk, which, no matter that he's currently drinking it, could be some kind of liquid explosive—and shove them into the X-ray machine. Soon we're trying to collapse the stroller while removing our shoes and holding on to a screaming kid. The helpful and patient TSA screener tells me to fold the stroller smaller even though it's already folded as compactly as possible. I enlighten him. The worker disagrees, responding that he's *sure* it can be made smaller, and could we please hop to it since we aren't the only people in line. I grind my teeth and cram the stroller into the machine. As we finally stagger through the metal detector, another TSA clone—who up until now has been lounging against a wall drinking Red Bull—saunters over just in time to confiscate our bottle of perfume and new tube of toothpaste. Someone's going to smell fresh after work tonight.

Nicholas is sucking in all the negative energy in the airport like a black hole with a pacifier, and as he wails impatiently, we know it's time to break out the cookies. It may be only be six thirty in the morning, but calling them "animal crackers" doesn't fool anyone, least of all Nicholas, who chortles happily at this turn of fortune and announces "Mama give tookie!" over and over. A momentary peace descends on us as we trudge beside the broken moving sidewalk all the way to gate 132Y. Through the grimy, graffitied windows, we catch glimpses of the sun's first rays shining through the haze.

In the gate lounge we receive the first of what will be a constant stream of evil stares. We know what people are thinking: *Please don't let that family with the baby sit near me!* We may as well be waiting to board the plane with SARS or a shoe bomb. Gangly teenagers plugged into iPods and businessmen with laptops are sitting in every third seat, so we plop down on carpet that's stained with unspeakable things and try to forget that we're about to enter a cramped, suffocating, metal tube with a squirming baby—voluntarily.

Putting on my best Bambi face, I ask the flight attendant at the counter if there are any empty seats and if she thinks there might be the *teeniest* chance that our sweet family will have a row to ourselves. She stops typing long enough to skewer me with her *you're about the eighth couple to ask me that* glare and say, "I'm sorry, but the flight is *completely* full." She's not nearly as sorry as I am.

Soon everyone else has boarded and it's time for "the walk." As we trespass in the rarified air of the first-class section, no one wastes a glance on us; people with diaper bags and milk-stained shirts aren't *their* kind of people. When we step into the cattle car, though, the passengers shift nervously in their pens. Anyone already sitting in a full row breathes a sigh of relief while those sitting in rows with empty seats get worried—one suddenly fiddles with the air vent, another spreads a winter jacket across the free seat as a last line of defense. We booked an aisle seat and a window seat, hoping for an empty middle seat, but up there on the right—row 22, seat B—we can see a thirty-something single guy who knows he's dead meat frantically mashing buttons on his Blackberry: *omg i hv 2 sit by a baby!!!* He offers to move over to the window seat.

At least the stewardess brings the packaged cookies—breakfast biscuits, if we can believe the wrapper—around soon. They're right up Nicholas's alley, so when the snack cart rolls by again, I snag six more packages from underneath. If each cookie buys five minutes of peace and quiet as Nicholas munches contentedly, then we'll need about seventy more cookies before we land.

The in-flight entertainment begins before takeoff, at least for Nicholas. It's now our job to keep him happy with a limited selection of toys for what is seemingly an unlimited amount of time. We've developed quite the repertoire, though: Slide the Ice Cube, Bang the Stir Stick, Stack the Cups, and, everyone's favorite, Rip the In-Flight Magazine. Today we begin with act one of "SkyMall Theater." *Look, Nicholas! Mr. Puppy walks UP the ramp into the DoggiePal Stroller that costs $189.99 but comes with a free UV-proof mosquito net!* Act two is interrupted by the *rrrrCLICK* of descending video screens as the in-flight entertainment begins for everyone else, and I feel a sharp longing for those days when in-flight stress was limited to choosing between a crossword puzzle and the latest Clive Cussler novel. Sure, Helen Mirren is a great actress, but there's something less than satisfying about watching *The Queen* with no sound in constantly interrupted two-minute segments.

Against all odds, Nicholas manages a short nap in my arms, perhaps the result of a post-sugar-rush crash. That gives me a chance to follow the movie for a while—*Oh! That guy isn't the butler; it's Tony Blair!*—but also causes both of my legs to fall fast asleep. My comfort level doesn't improve when the pimpled punk in front of me decides there probably won't be any sexy scenes with Princess Di and flings his seat backward. Luckily, my legs are so asleep that I can barely feel the cold ginger ale soaking into my crotch.

The overhead air vents begin to spread the odor of Nicholas's dirty diaper around the cabin. The tiny bathrooms on the plane don't have changing tables, so we have to do the job on our seats. As I take off Nicholas's diaper and spread his legs, I realize that there's no possible way this situation can be considered decent. "This one," I say to no one in particular, "is a five wiper."

Soon baby is clean and momentarily distracted by the final act of SkyMall Theater—*and that was when the Aqua-Zoom Robotic Pool Caddy brought Mama a* special *drink*—so I head back to the bathroom. I tug the door shut by its disconcertingly wet handle, and plop down on the closed toilet seat while the fluorescent lights flicker on. I'm too tired to pee. I'm too tired to think. I can only hope that these two minutes of silence will give me enough energy to make it to the end of this day. I breathe deeply, smelling the incongruous mixture of Lady Lilac hand soap and the last guy's bowel movement—truly a refreshing time.

But even this good thing must come to an end. The pilot wants everyone to *return to your seats*—either that or he wants everyone to *burn more meat*. As I walk back to row 22, the garbled announcement continues. *(click) Ahhhh. (click) This is your captain again. (click) It looks like, ah … (click) … we're being told that, ah … (click) … we may, ah, be encountering some, ah … (click) … patches of rough air, so … (click) … ah … (click) … it may be a bit … (click) … ah … (click) bumpy. (click)*

As the first tremors shake the cabin, Christine slides her air-sickness bag up in the seat pocket so that its sealable top and acid-proof wax liner are visible. She pats it reassuringly. The captain wasn't kidding about the rough air. The plane continues to shake as we descend toward the airport, and it's all Christine and I can do not to throw up on Nicholas's *I Spy* book that he wants us to read over and over: *I spy a race car, a red canoe, nauseous parents, and a barf bag, too!*

My forehead is bathed in sweat, and it feels like the pilot just turned on the heater. Suddenly, we hit the mother of all air pockets, and the plane drops like a roller coaster. Nicholas shoots into the air and his head connects with my jaw like an uppercut. Even our seat mate, who's been pretending to be asleep since we changed Nicholas's diaper, glances over with a wince, no doubt concerned by the apparent sound of my jawbone shattering. I'd smile reassuringly, but I'm pretty sure teeth or vomit would come out instead. So I continue to point to objects in the *I Spy* book ad nauseum, and I look out the window, praying that I'll soon see lights on the ground, since right now all I can see is the wing tip bouncing up and down like a teeter-totter.

And then a bone-jarring thunk tells us we're down. It's over. Christine smiles weakly at me. "We made it," I say to her. It's then we realize that we still have to taxi, wait to deplane, walk to the baggage claim, wait for our baggage, wait for the rental-car shuttle, wait for our rental car, install the car seat, and drive to our destination in the dark. We swear to each other that we'll *never* do this again, at least not until it's time to fly home in a few days' time.

Baby Love

My son is a real beauty, a fact that two Korean ladies pointed out last week. I was walking Nicholas to Happy Farm Produce, and coming toward us on the sidewalk were two middle-aged women. Rather than moving to one side in single file so we could pass each other, they stopped side-by-side and waited for me to close the distance. As I neared, I could see that they had eyes only for Nicholas, and he, who never says no to casual eye contact, was staring right back. As the woman on the left crouched to get a better view, the woman on the right exclaimed, "Oh! This is TV commercial baby!"

As I stood there, I felt like the pope's secretary, granting the favor of a brief audience with His Babiness. The women continued to stare and coo, and the one who was crouching made the inevitable observation about Nicholas's eyes being so blue and bright. She then stood to look at my eyes. After a quick appraisal and a confirming glance at Nicholas, she cocked her head and said, "*Mama* must be very beautiful!"

Christine and I, during our first months of parent-hood, often speculated on which of our parts had ended up with Nicholas. Our almost total ignorance regarding genetics and heredity gave us wide latitude. Clearly, he has Christine's eyes, so it's probable he won't have to bother with glasses like I do. Apart from the equipment that Nicholas needed from me to be male, we agreed he'd be better off getting almost everything else from Christine: perfect teeth, perfect eyes, strong thick hair, an effective immune system, and soft skin. "My son," I told him, "I don't have much to give, but what I have—my love for words and a bizarrely efficient metabolism—I give willingly."

Before Nicholas was born, the prospect of taking a baby on a walk would have petrified me, never mind the idea of holding one. I can remember once being forced to endure the trauma of holding a newborn. We met our friends Daniel and Marisa at a coffee shop, where it was agreed that I ought to hold newborn Jacob. The request—"Dave, do you want to hold the baby?"—was really a command. I was embarrassed and afraid. I thought everyone at the nearby tables would be watching my sad attempt, and I honestly feared that I might drop Jacob onto the floor. Could a baby die after falling from a lap? Might his head, which seemed so large and floppy, snap right off and roll under a neighboring table? I sat perfectly still for a few agonizing minutes. I failed entirely to notice the tiny person in my arms.

After Nicholas was born, I started to do things for him—changing diapers, giving sponge baths, rocking him to sleep, changing outfits, swaddling—and I noticed that he actually wasn't very breakable. In fact, he was downright resilient. I could hold him face down on one arm, like a living football. I could flip him, spin him, and move his arms and legs the way I wanted. This growing confidence had a side effect I hadn't anticipated. I began to know my baby. Like a scientist, I studied him from different angles. I held him underneath his arms, and my fingertips touched in the middle of his back. I handled his toes while I changed his diaper, toes so small that they were nearly impossible to grasp individually. I laid him on his stomach and ran my hand down his spine to watch his butt cheeks clench into dimples. I pulled him onto me to sleep and watched his full lips compress on the skin of my chest. I saw the way that water ran down his bulging belly as he took a bath in the sink. I had unrestricted access to Nicholas. As I grew intimately familiar with his body, I also grew in love.

This love for Nicholas's baby body soon transferred itself to other babies. Before Nicholas, I looked at a baby as a generic package, each one just like the next. Now I knew what to look for. If I had the chance to hold a new baby at church, I knew just the spot behind the ear to stick my nose for the best combination of softness and scent. I was comfortable staring into a baby's eyes from a foot away. Christine was amazed to hear me say that I couldn't wait to get my hands on a friend's newborn. I was amazed, too.

I recently said something else surprising: I don't want Nicholas to grow up. We have a very physical relationship, he and I, and we both know how it works. We connect on the level of touch. I hold him upside-down and tickle him, and when I stop he throws his head back for more. He clutches the string of my hoodie for security when I carry him into a strange place. At night, when he drinks his bottle in my arms, I trace my nose across the contours of his face; he runs his fingers all over mine. I kiss his forehead at the edge of his hair and let my lips stay there a moment to feel his skin.

What will become of us when Nicholas doesn't want me to kiss him anymore, or when my affection embarrasses him? Do I have nine years left? Three? When Christine and I were first married, I pictured her taking care of our kids until they were old enough to play soccer and ride a bike, and then I'd get involved. But now I discover that I am madly in love with Nicholas's chubby, soft, vigorous, beautiful body, and I don't want anything to change. I get this part of being a dad, but I'm scared of what comes next.

I like feeling certain of my son, and right now I do. When I walk through the front door in the evenings, Nicholas calls out from the other room, "Da-deee! Da-deee!" and I hear the *slap slap* of his hands on the wood floor as he crawls into the kitchen to see me. He'll find me as fast as possible so he can get tickled and hugged. This sometimes makes me grieve a loss that hasn't even happened yet — the first time Nicholas turns away from my embrace, or refuses my hand when I offer it to him. This refusal probably is a necessary step on his journey to manhood, but why can't that journey wait? Can't we stay here together on the floor, a happy heap of tickles and laughs, sure of this love that we know?

Lawn Care

When I was seventeen, my parents put me in charge of the house for a week. I was smart enough to confine my mess to a few rooms for easy last-minute cleaning. My parents assigned me only one real job: to keep the grass green. Our St. Augustine grass flourished in the summer heat of Southern California, but only if it received plenty of water. Automatic sprinklers, however, fail to notice tiny patches of dead grass that, if not attacked promptly with a hose, can spread quickly across the lawn. Into the gap steps the responsible homeowner, able and willing to tend the lawn, accepting the mission as part of the dramatic life of a WASP in the suburbs.

Pasadena is famous for its numerous trees, but even in the midst of all those trees, our backyard was an oasis. The lawn nestled against our L-shaped deck, its edges neatly trimmed into a series of graceful curves. Several small rises created a tri-level yard perfect for my brother, Rick, and me and all our friends. Ringing the grass were sections of deep ivy—into which base-balls and toys disappeared forever—sticky plumbago bushes, sturdy stands of oleander, fresh spearmint perfect for simulated chewing tobacco, and thick beds of agapanthus that shot their colorful cream and indigo fireworks into the air each summer.

Dad gave me careful instructions about how the grass ought to be watered. This wasn't a real-men-have-nice-lawns pissing contest; it was good old-fashioned Protestant work ethic. My dad—lieutenant, US Navy, retired—is a voracious worker. He expects hard work and wise stewardship from himself and his family. A green lawn is a good gift that ought to be tended and enjoyed.

Seventeen-year-olds aren't famous for a refined sense of responsibility, and I was no exception. What I'm still young enough to understand, though, is that the sometimes staggering irresponsibility of teenagers isn't usually motivated by malice. Or, for that matter, motivated by anything. Motivation is just too much work. Instead, teenagers usually take the path of least resistance, unless they happen to find the path of no resistance. In high school, for instance, there were many times that I decided not to cheat because it seemed like too much work.

It wasn't like I bore any ill will toward the lawn. I played football on it with my buddies. It was beautiful.

I liked when it was green. But searching out brown spots? Nightly watering? Mom and Dad could stand still and water one ten-by-ten-foot section of grass for twenty minutes or more. I, however, was a long way from *Zen and the Art of Lawn Care*. I could barely manage five minutes, all the while using the stream of water to trace patterns and funny words in the grass.

The day before my parents got back, I briefly stopped thinking about sports-girls-food-and-sleep. What I noticed was definitely not good. Several brown spots were spreading across the otherwise green lawn. These weren't tiny patches, either. They'd moved in for good, and they meant business. There was nothing for it but to hit those dead spots with everything I had. I spent more than double my normal time watering them. Ten minutes later, I turned the water off and rolled the hose up, my duty discharged.

The next day, I heard my parents arriving home, and I jogged outside to see them. After the usual round of hellos, hugs, and how-was-your-drive, we started to carry the bags into the house across the deck. That was when, from atop the deck, Dad let me know that the lawn was brown, that it was my fault, that I was a failure, and that I mattered to him less than the grass did.

At least that's what I felt like he said. I have no idea what he actually said; it was probably something reasonable like, "Dave, why is the lawn brown? Did you water it?" I probably responded by saying something cool and sarcastic like, "Wow, welcome home to you, too, Dad." (Conversations like this are why I plan on instituting a ban on talking in our home during Nicholas's teenage years.) Whatever the actual conversation, I felt sure that I had been unjustly attacked.

I'm almost thirty now, and I seem to have enough to fill my days without trying to relive the past. Dad has mellowed and brightened in the last decade. I've grown up. Let bygones be bygones. But then I realize that my bygones have come back for a visit. Nicholas is learning how to eat on his own, and our views about what that should look like differ. Nicholas thinks that feeding himself ought to involve license to throw any food that displeases him onto the floor or, if the fancy strikes him, at my head. I, on the other hand, believe that his food should go in his mouth or stay on his tray. In my efforts to lead him in the way I think he should go, I've made him cry, spectacularly and loudly, his lower lip curling toward the floor and tears rolling down his flushed cheeks. I can't know what he's thinking or feeling, but I have a sneaking suspicion that it might be a one-year-old version of what I felt that day on the deck with Dad.

But dinner needs to stay on the tray while it's eaten, and grass needs to stay green, and a thousand other things need to happen every day. So when a chunk of peanut butter sandwich hits my glasses and leaves a gooey streak down the right lens, I give Nicholas a time-out. I take his food away and turn his chair around. Nicholas begins to wail, and I listen while counting down a minute. I hear his cries; I see his little hands clench on the edge of his chair. I imagine what he would be saying to me if he could speak. Counting to sixty isn't easy. Most times, I feel like a jerk. Sometimes, after a particularly chaotic meal, I actually feel good about a time-out and the ensuing tears—*Don't you wish you'd listened to me earlier, Nicholas? Now you're getting what you deserve!*—and this makes me feel like an even bigger jerk.

But I'm realizing something that gets me through: discipline is an act of love. Nicholas is not in charge of his own life, nor should he be. Christine and I are there to teach Nicholas how to live, which frustrates him when he wants to survive on applesauce and graham crackers. We're teaching Nicholas his place in the order of things, and because of those lessons, he's also learning that he can trust us to take care of him when things go wrong. This is the same kind of navy-style love my dad had for me that summer afternoon in our backyard. My dad knew—as do I, now—that keeping the lawn green isn't so different from keeping food on your plate.

It's one thing to look into my past and, because of my own experience as a parent, gain a new vision for what my parents were trying to teach me. It's something totally different to look at my present with any kind of clarity, or to know how to discipline *myself*. Christine and I have unwittingly begun to examine our consciences as we lay in bed at night, a la St. Ignatius of Loyola. Ignatius learned that it's a good idea to think through what you've done each day, and then imagine how you can do better tomorrow. For us, it's natural to talk about Nicholas each night — the cute phrases he said, the new skills he learned, and how badly he was acting when he threw that toy against the side of the piano. Usually, as we talk through a situation, we agree: either we handled it well or we didn't, and then we help each other think of what to do differently next time.

For example, we've been trying to teach Nicholas how to use the phone, a project hampered by the fact that he can't really talk and doesn't know what a phone is and has only the haziest of notions regarding object permanence. These hurdles notwithstanding, our goal is to get Nicholas to be able to listen to his grandma's voice on the phone and then say something suitably endearing like, "Wuv-oo, gammah!" This isn't a selfless project, admittedly, since we know that the amount of cool presents he'll receive the next time he sees Grandma is proportional to the number of cute comments he makes on the phone.

Right now, though, all Nicholas can manage to do is babble his head off right up until the moment we hold the phone to his ear, at which point his face transforms into a decent impression of a drooling idiot. His eyes focus in the distance as Grandma's hypnotic words wash over him. Our pleas to say something fall on deaf ears, or maybe on ears already too full of the blissful sound of Grandma's voice to hear anything else. We've had mixed success with tricking Nicholas into talking on the phone by holding it where he can't see it and hoping that Grandma will still hear him, but then he can't hear her, of course. We have to face facts: despite our hopes, Nicholas may not grow up to be a successful telemarketer.

In bed that night, Christine and I laugh at how Nicholas loves the *concept* of talking on the phone, but his execution needs a lot of work, and at the fact that there may come a day, all too soon, on which we have to lecture Nicholas to spend *less* time talking on the phone. I'm a tiny bit frustrated, though; I ask Christine why Nicholas, since he loves his grandma and knows how to say a lot of words, can't just put two and two together and say a few words to Grandma *on the phone?* Couldn't he make just a little effort?

That's about when Ignatius strolls into the room. *David, could you remember to call your aunt Millie this week sometime?* Well, yes, I could remember, but I probably won't because I just can't be bothered to pick up the phone and have a pleasant conversation. I make

Christine take care of the family business on the phone if at all possible, forcing her to call the bank, the insurance company, and so on. Sometimes when her sister calls and I'm reading, I'll check the caller ID and let the answering machine pick up. I can go for months without talking to my brother or my friends on the phone.

What else, I wonder, do I suck at? More politely, what else is Nicholas learning that I need to learn as well? It's a list that's surprisingly easy to generate: learning to be nice, learning that the world doesn't revolve around me, learning to share, learning to wait. The more I think about it, the more I realize that Nicholas's lessons are my lessons. Nicholas has two parents who outweigh him and who are willing to give him a time-out when he needs to learn a lesson. On the other hand, I weigh the same as myself, and when I need a time-out, I tend to bring my own beer and sit in front of a Lakers game. Guess who's going to learn his lessons faster?

When did I forget this stuff? When you move out of your parents' home, do you leave all your lessons behind? I know I *used* to be pretty disciplined—the stereotypical good kid. I didn't get in trouble at school. One of the saddest stories I know about myself, and one I hope will never be told of Nicholas, is this: when I was in second grade, my parents were called in to speak with my teacher, who gravely informed them that I was a bit too compliant, and was there perhaps something they weren't telling her about my situation? I can just imagine having a conversation with Nicholas about this in the future: "Nicholas, I know what it's like to get in trouble. You see, when I was your age, I got in trouble."

"What for, Dad?"

"What for? Oh, er, well … for being too obedient."

"Wow, Dad, you really were a bad kid, weren't you!"

"Okay, wipe that smirk off your face, Junior!"

Somewhere along the way I forgot a whole bunch, or else I decided that certain rules didn't apply to me anymore. It's embarrassing to admit, but Nicholas is better at sharing than me. He isn't perfect, by any stretch of the imagination. There are certain toys that hold a special place in Nicholas's heart, and trying to borrow one is tantamount to deep betrayal in his eyes. Most of the time, though, he seems to like sharing. It's common to hear him saying, "Mama's turn! Nicholas's's turn!" (He's absorbing the grammatical structures of English scary-fast, but possessives still bedevil him.)

Not so for me, though. As Christine can attest, one of the quickest ways to get me in a bad mood is to take a sip of my soda—*I needed* exactly *twelve ounces!* I don't like sharing my time, my food, my space, or my energy. I don't want to kid myself; I know that Nicholas won't always like to share. And he doesn't have to, either. He'll learn, as I have, that sometimes you need to share things if you want to be part of polite society. You don't always have to like it, but you always have to be willing to do it.

There's another issue, though, a deeper kind of sharing. A kind of sharing that I fail at every day. When Christine and I first moved in with my parents, we knew we'd be living with them for about a year. We were determined to make the most of our time together, knowing it was only temporary. I decided I'd do all sorts of things to bond with my parents—have dinner with them regularly, have a night out with my dad a couple of times a month, share a brownie and a bit of conversation with my mom. And what I've found is that those things demand a willingness to share myself—my time, my energy, my feelings—that I either can't or won't muster.

This is troubling. I'd like to be putting energy into my adult relationships, of course. But what troubles me even more is the possibility that I might begin relating to Nicholas in the same way, and that I might teach him to relate to me that way, too. Every time I choose to say, distractedly, "Huh? Oh, wow ..." to one of his comments instead of, "You worked hard building that tall tower, Nicholas," I'm taking the low-energy approach. How soon before that begins feeding back from Nicholas to me? Sure, I expect it when he's a surly teenager, but hopefully not when he's in preschool. "What's that, Dad? Oh, ah, maybe I'll play cars with you later ... I'm kinda into this movie here."

As odd as it may sound, Nicholas is a role model for me. Not in everything, mind you—I don't really want to burst into tears when I have to leave the park before I want to. But when it comes to knowing how to wait, Nicholas inspires me. Waiting, you see, is *really* hard for Nicholas. The kid has no concept of time. Anything in the past is "yesterday," while anything in the future is "in a few more minutes." We still want to help him learn to wait for certain things, though, like waiting to eat dinner until after the food is cooked, or waiting to go to the zoo until after he wakes up in the morning. So I tell him things like, "Honey, play cars for a few more minutes while I cook your oatmeal," and he responds with something like, "Nicholas eat oatmeal Nicholas eat oatmeal Nicholas eat oaaaatmeaaaal!"

But here's what I admire about the way he waits: Nicholas keeps his eyes on the prize when it comes to waiting for Things That Matter. Sure, when he's waiting to get into the car to go somewhere, I can distract him with a movie while I get dressed. When he's waiting for something essential, though, like food or a hug and kiss before bed, *nothing* stands in his way. He keeps asking and asking and asking until he gets it, and he's not above bursting into tears, screaming, or taking matters into his own tiny hands.

This single-minded pursuit of good things shames me. So often I get things doubly backward, chasing things that don't matter while steadfastly refusing to fight for what does. It's surfing the web instead of calling a friend. It's the dead-end repetition of doing what I don't *really* want to and failing to do what I should. It's being human, I think—not that that makes it any easier to take. I can make a list of what, deep down, I value—like relationships, new experiences, growth—and what I actually spend my time on—like television, computer games, and lazing around. It doesn't take a two-year-old to notice the contrast.

When I began to have the freedom to make my own decisions, I took that freedom and ran with it, running all the way into the arms of myself. Every bit and byte of information in the cultural air reinforces this, urging me farther and farther into a self-defined future in which I exist at the center of a universe with a population of one. Nicholas, though, remains firmly connected to the people around him, and, as a result, he can't help but grow and learn. He's part of a community—his family—that has dreams for his growth and betterment, and—this is crucial—that community holds him accountable for those dreams. My problem is that as an adult I don't *have* to be accountable. I'm accountable only when I place myself willingly in situations that force me to expose my hopes and fears to others who love me and want to help me grow. That's infinitely harder than watching TV, and who wants things to get harder? It's a lot easier to cut myself slack, time and time again. Too much slack, though, and I'm not attached to anything.

On my favorite TV show, *The Office*, Steve Carell plays the boss, Michael Scott, a man crippled by narcissism and ego. This leads to such gems as "Would I rather be feared or loved? Easy—both. I want people to be afraid of how much they love me." On a recent episode, as he hid from a brownnosing underling, Michael faced the camera and said, "I don't understand how someone can have *so little* self-awareness."

What self-awareness I do have is forced upon me— through my writing, my marriage, and my son—but how can I have *so little?* And how can I be aware of problems and then do nothing to fix them? Nicholas and I are learning how to talk on the phone, eat politely, and say please; basically, we're learning what it means to be in relationship, what it means to be human. We're learning that we exist not as islands in the middle of a selfish sea but as fingers interlaced in community. Sometimes that means he can't throw food at dinner, even if that loss makes him cry. Sometimes that means I can't avoid calling Aunt Millie. And sometimes it means that I have to stand up, turn off the television, and take my dad out for coffee, even if I have to pay. After all, with enough water, any lawn can become green again.

Domestic

If I could have glimpsed, as a college student, one of my current days, I would have collapsed in a blubbering heap. Up at 6:00 AM? Full-time work *and* full-time parenting? *Diapers?!?* Such things would have been as unimaginable as other mythical grown-up activities like cooking dinner and ironing. As a single eighteen-year-old, I figured that having a kid meant things would proceed pretty much normally, except for the baby hanging out unobtrusively somewhere nearby. If a south swell was hitting the coast, then baby could read on a beach towel while daddy paddles out. Now, of course, I know that scenario is ridiculous—babies can't read!

As I approach the beginning of my fourth decade, though, my normal life seems, well, normal. Instead, it's life before Nicholas that's unimaginable. A friend and fellow parent told me that she recently slept past 7:00 AM for the first time in over three years. (Sweet—I'm halfway to *my* first sleep-in!) That's the way things go when you're a parent. You contort your life to accommodate a new person who will do things differently than you do. And as you stretch and rearrange yourself for someone else—by learning to think happy thoughts while you change a wet diaper, wet pajamas, and wet bedding in the middle of the night, for example—you begin to see your life in a new way.

Take free time, for instance. My free time used to be all about me and what I wanted to do, whether it was go for a long run or watch a basketball game on TV. Now that I'm a dad, though, my free time is all about Nicholas, since his free time requires constant parental involvement. So instead of doing something I wanted to do on a rainy Thursday in Vancouver, I found myself playing magnets, which is an alluringly simple game: Nicholas takes all the letter magnets off the fridge and carries them one by one to the "Tax Documents" file drawer of our desk, where he dumps the magnets, and then I carry all the magnets back to the fridge and stick them up again. It's not that this game wasn't fun the first time, or even the eighth time, but eventually I tried to persuade Nicholas to do something else, something we could both agree on.

In the Pacific Northwest (Canadians, naturally enough, think of Vancouver as the temperate *South*west), rain doesn't stop you from doing anything; it just means that you always carry a fleece and a hat. So I ask Nicholas if he wants to go play at the abandoned railroad tracks down the block, which is something I'd never do on my own but now do almost daily in the company of my always-curious baby.

Just traversing the half-block from our place to the tracks is worthy of a Discovery Channel special. First comes the grueling ascent of the five steps outside the front door of our basement apartment. Nicholas grunts and pants as he labors up the steep slope, while I, the faithful Sherpa, carry our gear. We reach the top only to confront the gate. For a toddler, every gate has a 50 percent chance of being unopenable, because, of course, half the time the gate opens toward the toddler, who is standing smack in the way of its opening. Nicholas feels pretty clever, since he knows where the latch on this gate is, but his pride is quickly revealed as hubris when he thunks the gate confidently into his forehead. Undeterred, he repeats this procedure several more times. I've actually seen him open the gate this way, since the continual bashing from the gate scoots him back an inch or so each time. Today, though, I open the gate for him, and he rambles through, highly pleased with himself.

When we finally reach the street, I pick up Nicholas and turn my body exaggeratedly to the left. "Any cars?" I ask Nicholas. "Okaaay!" he replies. "No," I say, "there aren't any cars. Say 'No cars.'" "Okaaay!" says Nicholas.

We navigate beneath an overhanging blackberry bush that looks like it would love to tangle itself in Nicholas's hair, and at last we arrive at the tracks, our view opening up for hundreds of yards in either direction along the straight-as-an-arrow rails.

We turn right and amble toward the new townhouse development where Nicholas loves to gape at the "nonnies" (short, in baby talk, for "construction vehicles"). Today there are two excavators scooping up shovelfuls of dirt *and* dumping them into waiting dump trucks—high drama in the city. Nicholas wants up for a better view, and once he's up, he confirms what we're seeing: "Nonnies! Trucks! Biiiig!" The driver of the larger, yellow excavator gives us a wave, and I wave Nicholas's arm back. I wonder if my mom waved my arm at burly construction workers when I was a toddler, and if that has something to do with why I'm such an introvert now. Content that the construction is proceeding per his wishes, Nicholas wants down. I lower him to the path beside the tracks with a grunt, and there we both stand. This—looking at stuff, standing around—is what I do a lot nowadays.

Soon the sun shows its face, and I sit down on one of the rails. From the space between the ties I grab two small, gray rocks and place them side by side on the rail nearest Nicholas. He gets the hint and starts to play his second-favorite outside game, something I call Line Up the Rocks and he calls Rocks. He cobbles together a line of five or so rocks before his arm begins to knock off the old rocks each time he places a new one. He's stuck in an endless loop, and loving it. I wouldn't characterize my own thoughts so generously, though. Sure, the first time your kid stacks rocks in a line you contemplate his genius and begin to think of ways to pay for his four years at MIT. But after the fiftieth time, your eyes sort of glaze over, and while your body continues to help stack rocks and say "wow" every few seconds, your brain leaps into a hammock and begins to dream.

I picture our family vacations each summer when I was young. Whenever the smog and heat of Los Angeles hit unbearable levels, we'd drive to a national park, get out of the car, and start chucking rocks at stuff. A petrified tree in central Oregon, a bit of moss hanging from a nurse log in Washington's Olympic Peninsula rainforest, a small stick bobbing down the rippled waters of a creek in Glacier National Park: all legitimate targets for two baseball-obsessed brothers. I can only hope that I've inherited a fraction of my parents' genius for keeping kids occupied. "First one to hit this piece of driftwood"— and Dad would do his discus-thrower imitation, lobbing a flat piece of wood out over the rippling surface of the lake, where it slapped the surface of the water like a flat palm— "with five rocks gets dessert tonight." We'd arc stone after stone through the air, occasionally hitting the wet surface of the drifting wood with a satisfying *clack* and mentally choosing our just desserts.

The sun disappears behind a cloud, and the sudden shift of light recalls me to the present. Nicholas is asking over and over to play his first-favorite game, something I call Throw Rocks at Random and he calls Rocks. He gives the game his full concentration, and so do I. He usually manages little better than a two-foot plop, but every so often he gets lucky and wings a rock with enough force to do damage, so I have to stay alert. Sitting behind him is no guarantee of safety, either. His rocks scatter around us, but I take aim at bigger game, lobbing my rocks at the nearest telephone pole, which I manage to hit *way* more often than Nicholas. I peg it ten times before he even hits it once.

That's right: I'm competing with my baby. This isn't strange; it's standard behavior for most guys. And so is the desire to win, even if it's against a person who barely reaches my knees and poops in his pants several times a day. I've always been a good sport, and by that I mean that I've always been good *at* sports, not that I've been nice. In elementary school I made a younger girl cry when I beat her at ping-pong and then gloated. (I swear I thought she could handle it, since she was a tough Montana farm girl. She got her revenge the next day, though, when I had to ride in her dad's combine and watch the bile-inducing number of grasshoppers that were collected in the back of the harvester along with the wheat. That's why I'm strictly a bleached-flour guy—for my health.)

Wanting to beat Nicholas at rock tossing is just par for the male course, and considering the rate at which my athletic skills are atrophying and the corresponding rate at which his are growing, I figure that I have only a few more years of domination. It's important for him to beat me eventually, though. The son succeeds the father, the apprentice becomes the master. In the defining myth of our age, it's Obi-Wan letting Darth Vader strike him down so that Luke can become a Jedi. Or it's Professor Dumbledore training Harry Potter, and then forcing Harry to watch him die—the only way to make sure that Harry comes into his own as a wizard. I don't plan on getting light-sabered anytime soon, or falling victim to the *Avada Kedavra* curse, but I do need to figure out how to let Nicholas succeed me. I'm scared that I won't have the courage to let Nicholas become his own person, his own man, and that I'll try to prolong his dependence on me. Every day, every time he learns something new, this fear is present. I like being needed.

One thing that Nicholas certainly still needs me for is walking uphill. Nicholas maintains a healthy respect for hills—for him, every hill, from a mountain to a one-foot ramp, is *steeeep!* I don't know whether it's just a skill he hasn't yet learned, or it's the big-head, short-legs thing he has going on, but hills are trouble. He's constantly on the verge of falling backward and, I imagine, tumbling down and breaking his crown while I come chasing after.

When we moved to Santa Barbara, hills became a constant part of his life. So as we go for a walk around our neighborhood on a wintry day—mostly sunny and in the sixties—I carry him up the first hill. Walking with Nicholas is an exercise in spiritual discipline. Touring our cul-de-sac at the rate of one house every ten minutes makes me hop up and down with impatience; hearing Nicholas ask "Cat?" for the twelfth time in a row makes me want to scream—*Of course it's a cat; what part of this noun thing aren't you getting?* But how could I stay mad at him? Hearing his happy hoot when he manages to "pet" (whack) our neighbor's cat reminds me what we're up to. I do my best saint imitation—"Not my will be done, but yours," I tell Nicholas. He looks up at me and smiles. "Cat?"

Our walk is packed with things to do and see, things I don't usually notice, like the little path around a certain birdbath that makes a perfect place to run, or the small orange circle of spray paint on the sidewalk down the street. When I speed by these things in my car, I never pay attention to them. However, now that Nicholas totters around the path over and over, or stoops to trace the circle with his finger time and again, I can't help but observe them in great detail. Exhaustive detail. Excruciating detail. Let's not romanticize paths or painted circles: when I drove past them before, I wasn't missing much. Sometimes seeing the world through the eyes of a child makes me glad to have the eyes of an adult. What Nicholas helps me adjust is not my sight but my mindset, my habit of speeding through life. He helps me slow down. Sometimes *way* down, like when I have to carry his chubby little butt back uphill to our house.

Some things Nicholas hasn't developed yet feel like blessings. For example, Nicholas is utterly unself-conscious. Having the self-consciousness of an adult is something I'd chuck without a second thought. I'm convinced that we still suffer the same kind of crippling insecurities that made middle school and high school such psychic train wrecks, but we insulate ourselves by spending less time in the school lunchroom and more time eating in our cars. Today Nicholas is practicing spin jumps on a neighbor's lawn, apparently deciding to skip right past normal walking. Spin jumps, at least as I demonstrate them for Nicholas, consist of jumping in place while twisting in a complete lateral circle. If you want a good picture of what spin jumps look like for Nicholas, imagine the way that a dog leaping for a frisbee twists its body in the air, but then take away the dog's inner ear. As Nicholas picks himself up off the grass, he shouts, "Daddy turrrrn!" It's then that I notice a lady watching us through her miniblinds, and suddenly I'm back in junior high. Now, though, Nicholas is the cool kid, the one I want to please, so when he says jump, I ask, "How many spins?"

Almost home, we trundle into the driveway just below our house. Nicholas wants to say hi to the stone pelican that's forever perching on a piling on this front porch. Nicholas doesn't have a lot of social skills, so I help him out. "Say 'hi' to the pelican, honey." He shifts from one foot to the other, considering the statue, before saying, "Hi, peckin." "Do you want to pat the pelican?" I ask. He climbs up onto the front step so that he can reach the bird's head, and I hear his small hand slapping lightly on the smooth stone. "Nice peckin bird, nice peckin bird," he breathes over and over.

Now that I'm a dad, I talk to stone animals and pretend to care about spray-painted circles on the sidewalk. It's enough to drive me crazy, but the thing that's really crazy is that these things have started to matter to me. I'm sure it wouldn't take too long to get back into the groove of selfishness when it comes to my free time, but as long as Nicholas needs me, I'll keep walking around our cul-de-sac, looking for cats and practicing my spin jumps.

• • •

Domestic

I haven't tried to look cool for years, maybe even decades. Looking slovenly isn't a failing on my part, though—it's a way to test how cool everyone else is. If you care that I look bad, then you are too shallow to be worth knowing. Aren't I just *so* deep? Unfortunately, this cavalier attitude toward fashion (and, to be honest, hygiene) isn't one that my wife is allowing me to pass on to Nicholas. So when it comes time for me to get Nicholas dressed for the park, I dutifully dress him in something that I'm pretty sure matches. Dressing Nicholas is not something I ever attempt unless I am willing either to (a) follow my wife's instructions explicitly and uncomplainingly or (b) endure my wife's withering stare and comments like, "I hope you didn't take him to the park in *that*." ("That," uttered in this context, is a stand-in for the phrase "that outfit, which, by the mindblowing extent of its inappropriateness, screams to all the world that I am a bad mother for allowing my son to be seen wearing it in public, even if it was, thank goodness, only with *you*, you slob!")

All things considered, just saying "in *that*" is much preferred. And what—purely hypothetically—is so wrong about wearing white shorts, a jammie shirt with oatmeal stains on it, and slip-on dress shoes to the park when it's sixty degrees out? As I pull on a one-piece play outfit over Nicholas's head (no mistakes possible here, except in the shoe, jacket, and possibly hat

139

departments), I comfort myself with the thought that Christine would never be able to pick an appropriate utility player for my fantasy basketball team when I'm behind in both blocks and free-throw percentage for the week. She's not the only one with valuable skills to teach Nicholas! It's odd that now, after years and years of paying little attention to what I wear, I find myself thinking things like *Nicholas's sailboat Robies would look* much *cuter with this outfit.* While Nicholas may not care about my new clothing chops, I know that Christine does.

Once dressed, it's park time. The park is Nicholas's favorite place ever, even topping the zoo. I have a feeling that the only place he might like better would be one of those indoor play-gyms like they have at Chuck E. Cheese (or Up-Chuck E. Cheese, as my uncle calls it), but we'd never take Nicholas there; those ball pits are like the bacterial Fertile Crescent. Nicholas has his parks categorized by the color of the play equipment: brown (Hidden Valley Park), green (La Mesa Park), and blue (Shoreline Park) are his favorites. So when I ask him if he wants to go to the park, he says, "Um … green!" Where did my kid, like, learn to use, um, filler words?

Getting in the car to go somewhere with a baby can make me feel like I'm in *Sophie's Choice.* I think I've got everything—snacks, drinks, diapers, wipes, sand toys, toys for the car, Hot Wheels, a sweater, a phone, a wallet—and Nicholas is belted into his car seat, when I notice that I've left the front door open. What to do? Take a happy baby out of his car seat and go shut the door? Or leave him in the car seat while I shut the door, giving some lunatic the chance to drive off with my baby? I settle for jogging backward to the door, facing the car the whole time so I can leap at any would-be kidnapper with my catlike reflexes.

As for our actual time at the park, read the following out loud: *Slide! Wheeee! Again!* Now repeat it forty-six times while you stand in the sun and try to look excited, all the while lifting a thirty-pound sack of potatoes above your head. Oh, and make sure your gut has that "I just *know* we're going to end up in the emergency room" feeling in it. There, you've just spent an afternoon at the park. I used to consider parks as places either to play soccer with my buddies or have a romantic picnic with my lady. Now? It's all about the slides, baby.

When Nicholas avoids serious injury for forty-five minutes, it's time to count our blessings and head home. The perfect car ride starts with the perfect music. For Nicholas, this means one of his inane kids' CDs, on which the children all sing with British accents and the lead singer sounds like she's wearing too much perfume and has lipstick smudged on her teeth. While listening to music at home, Nicholas always performs his best—and only—dance move, spinning in a circle like a whirling dervish until he topples onto the carpet. In the car, though, strapped tightly into his car seat, the best movement Nicholas can manage is a side-to-side rock that's guaranteed to be out of sync with the music. (You're welcome, Son.) "Aye-Aye-O!" demands Nicholas as I start the car, asking for his *Zoo Train* album, on which a delightful little blue train full of happy children chugs its way through a magical zoo for an excruciating hour. I hate those kids. As soon as I start the song, Nicholas begins to belt out, "Hooray zoo!" in a monotone, sounding exactly like Will Ferrell with a voice immodulation disorder. I sing along loudly with the CD—"Hooray for the zoo today!"—hoping to help Nicholas catch on to the concept of melody. The only thing *I* catch, though, is a funny look from the teenager getting into his car beside me.

Music is a big part of my life, too, but I seem to be fighting a losing battle with a tiny person whose music makes me want to cram pacifiers into my ears. I'm still not okay with the idea of surrendering my musical autonomy, and I try to get Nicholas to see things my way. "Daddy is going to listen to *his* music," I tell Nicholas, to which he yells, "Aye-Aye-O!" "Do you want to hear what electric guitar sounds like," I ask him, "or NPR?" This time he thinks a little, bouncing in his car seat. He smiles and yells, "Zoo!"

As the nasally kids trill on and on about the funny, fuzzy monkeys who are having so much fun, we pull into traffic, and Nicholas informs me that he wants— nay, *needs*—a drink. Since his sippy cup is empty, I give him my water bottle. That's like someone handing me a five-gallon bucket of water to drink from and then sending me on a roller coaster. Soon Nicholas is soaked, with perhaps 95 percent of the water on his clothes and 5 percent in his mouth. The only part of him that's *dry*, by this point, is his diaper. He doesn't seem to mind, though. "Did you take drinks from the water bottle like a big boy?" I ask him. "By self!" he trumpets. Why this should make me proud I can't say, but proud is what I feel.

The rest of the ride home is filled with new discoveries. "What's'at?" asks Nicholas, and I tell him it's a cherry-picker truck. "What's'at?" asks Nicholas, and I tell him it's a tandem bicycle. "What's'at?" asks Nicholas, and I remind him that it's the same cherry-picker truck that I pointed out ten seconds earlier. He smiles. "Two trucks!" he yells.

And then, as we near home, we happen upon Nicholas's first crush, his constant flame, his one-and-only baby love: the fire station. Wouldn't you know it? Both engines are parked in the driveway this evening, paint and chrome gleaming in the reddening sunlight. I see Nicholas in the mirror, hopping up and down in his seat, enraptured. If his life stopped now, he would have experienced a peak of joy as lofty as any human in history. He's beyond words. As I turn my eyes back to the road, I catch sight of myself in the mirror, and *I'm* grinning ear to ear just like my son. Why? Because two fire engines are parked outside the fire station? Well, yeah, actually. That *is* why.

I know less than I used to. Being a dad makes me dumber—between the lack of sleep, the idiotic songs, the toxic smells, and the constant communication with someone who can barely talk, there's no way around it. But I *feel* more. And more deeply, too. As we drive past the fire station, the chorus from U2's "City of Blinding Lights" pops into my head loud and clear, one of those moments when life has a soundtrack. I mute the zoo train and look in the mirror at Nicholas, who's kicking his feet with happiness. "Hey Nicholas," I say, and as he looks at me, I sing:

> And I miss you when you're not around
> I'm getting ready to leave the ground
> Oh, you look so beautiful tonight

If I could have known what my life as a young dad would *look* like, I might have tried to avoid the whole getting-married-having-kids thing. There's just no way that I would have signed up for the requisite rock-stacking and gate-opening courses. Luckily for me, though,

I didn't have that prescience, and instead I lucked into the gift of fatherhood, like when you're camping and you wake up at exactly the right moment to see the best sunrise in the history of the world. If I could have *felt* what life would be like as a dad, though, I would have longed to jump right in. More than feeling bored or tired or trapped, I feel this as a dad: a singular joy in being needed and wanted by my son, a joy I wouldn't trade for anything I felt before I became a father. And there's this, too: seeing fire trucks makes me, a grown man, happily sing at the top of my lungs. When I take another look at my son in the mirror, his joy—body humming, eyes wide enough to drink his whole shining world—is a blinding light. I'm a dad now, and it's the only life that I can want or imagine.

Anger Management

It's a sunny Saturday morning, and I'm pushing Nicholas's stroller into an intersection while chatting with Christine. The light is green, and as we step into the crosswalk, a pickup turns right in front of us, missing the stroller by only a few feet. I jerk the stroller back and Christine yells at the driver, who, deciding to compound his idiocy, yells back at *us* for not watching where *we* are going. "We have a green light!" screams Christine, her voice cracking and her hand smacking the side of the truck as it whips past us. I turn back to face the fleeing driver, and as I flip him off, I notice that my hand is shaking.

Understandable reactions, to be sure. What's less understandable is what I do next: I hide my anger from Christine and tell *her* to calm down. "It's no big deal," I say. "We're all safe. Let it go." Since then, I've tried to discover a reason for the way I acted. Why didn't I let myself experience that anger or admit it to Christine?

What was I afraid of? Surely I had a right to be angry, and yet I acted like everything was fine and dandy.

If avoiding my anger is a problem for me, other times I find myself embracing anger when there's really nothing to be angry about. Recently I was driving with my dad. I stopped a few feet over the line at a red light, and my dad used the opportunity to give me a lecture: "Dave, come on! You stopped way over the line—that's dangerous!" Bristling, I ran through a list of defenses in my head: I'm not that far past the line; our light is about to turn green anyway; there isn't a sidewalk, so I'm not endangering any pedestrians. Something that diffused the tension ever so effectively escaped my lips: "Dad, gimme a break; I've been driving for ten years without any accidents or tickets!" We bickered for a while, both of us our righteous selves, and finally solved the problem by talking about something else. Throughout the rest of the day, whenever I thought of what my dad said, I got angry all over again. I savored the experience of coming up with biting responses that would have shown him who was right and who was wrong.

And then there are the times I'm most unhappy with how I handle my anger: the times when I'm angry with my son. "Mama chaaaange diaperrrr!" The pitiful, heartrending screech drills into my eardrums. Nicholas's screaming, saliva-covered lips are just inches from my face, and I stare for a moment at the little hangy thing at the back of his throat. Just now it's shaking like a leaf in the wind.

"Mama chaaaange diaperrrr!" Nicholas's whole body is getting into the act. He stiffens his spine and arches backward. He beats his tiny fists and kicks his legs together like a demon-dolphin, accompanied by a fresh round of screams that makes me wonder if he's doing permanent damage to his vocal chords. Or to my eardrums.

I'm starting to get upset. I can change diapers with the best of 'em, so Nicholas's insistence on his mother is making me feel rejected and unloved. "Hey. Stop. Daddy's going to change your diaper." As we head into the bedroom, with Nicholas starting to shed tears (crocodile tears, I tell myself), I can feel my anger rising. Struggling to stay in control, I try to be reasonable. "Sometimes Mama changes your diaper, and sometimes Daddy does. We take turns." Not convinced by my logic, Nicholas continues to ask for Mom. Even though I know Nicholas sometimes asks for *me* when Christine changes his diaper, I still feel hurt, and part of me— please let it be a small, small part—wants to hurt my baby back.

I could go on and on—my days are filled with anger of all kinds. From the righteous anger I deny to the petty anger I indulge to the scary-dark anger I can feel toward my son, it seeps through the cracks in my brittle shell.

It's painful to consider; this isn't the kind of person I want to be. I seem like a stranger to myself: who am I to be pissed at my baby? Who am I — a supposedly kind husband, loving dad, and devoted son — who am I to let comments about my driving make me grip the steering wheel so tightly that my knuckles turn white? There are plenty of things in the world worth getting angry about, so why do I rage at the wrong ones?

One obvious conclusion from these stories is that I can be a world-class jerk. Denying my wife's emotions and my own, snapping at my dad, and wanting to hurt my child aren't credentials for my Dad of the Year application. I don't resist this conclusion, either; a little self-loathing is probably a good thing from time to time. I wish I could blame the cruel world for my problems, but I can't; they come from the darkness inside me. Jesus once chided a bunch of blockheads about this: *Are you crazy? You think it's what goes* into *you that makes you dirty? Come on, it's the crap that comes* out *that you should be worried about!*

That's exactly what scares me. If I'd been holding a coffee mug when that pickup almost ran us over, would I have thrown it through the back window? If the driver had stopped, would I have cursed him? What would have happened if one of us threw a punch? And what if my dad had made one more comment about my driving? What if Nicholas had asked for his mom to change his diaper just one more time? Would I have yelled at him? Physically hurt him? It's gut-wrenching to write about these possibilities; after all, I'm talking about legal felonies here, not to mention serious moral failings. As Jim Carrey admits in *Liar Liar*, "I hold *myself* in contempt!"

This isn't a healthy place to conclude, though. I figure too much self-loathing will only make things worse; like a plant given too much water, I'll weaken and drown beneath waves of regret and condemnation. So what's the solution? Holding myself in contempt doesn't really solve anything, and since I'm a guy, solving things is what I'm all about. I can't sit around analyzing myself. I still have to take walks and change Nicholas's diaper and every so often drive my dad somewhere. I want to know that I can do those simple things without doing something that I'll regret.

When Nicholas gets bogged down by his negative emotions, I try to help him see that there's a better way to do things. If he's being a pill, I ask him if he can think of a nicer way to act. Then, after he comes up with something, I reset the situation and help him role-play his way through it, but this time as a kid with good manners. He seems to latch on to this; he's much more likely to be polite in a given situation once he's practiced how to do it. I don't really think that I need to drive my parents around and around the city, waiting for the chance to practice a healthy reaction. I've always had a good imagination, so maybe that's where I should begin.

I carry Nicholas into his room one night to start our bedtime routine. He insists on reading books with Mama—his current favorite—and I get irritated. But c'mon, he's not even two! He's just a little guy, as I frequently tell him, and now I remind myself of that fact. He craves the security of fulfilled expectations, and he wants to know that he's in control of certain parts of his life. Turns out we're pretty similar! I remind myself that Nicholas loves me. I rub his back and tell him that I know he wanted to read with Mama and that he might feel a little sad. And while he adjusts to reading with me, I carry him outside to look at the moon, which looks like a fingernail flicked into the dark sky. Nicholas perks up, telling me, "Moon is half circle!" We head inside and walk slowly down the hall to his bedroom, his small hand resting on my shoulder like we're waltzing. As Nicholas snuggles into my lap to read about construction vehicles, I close my eyes and concentrate on the smell of his hair. I don't need to look to know what's coming next.

A few weeks later, I'm driving my parents home from a party. It's a clear night with light traffic, and the ideal driving conditions aren't even dampened by wondering when my dad will comment on my driving. I expect it, actually, and I already know what I'll say: "Yep, thanks for the reminder." This comment is respectful and easy. I'm talking about the man who helped give me life and raise me, for goodness' sake; I don't need to sass him about traffic rules! So what if I was already doing what he asks. What do I want, a merit badge? So when I hear, "Dave, are you signaling when you change lanes?" I smile to myself, count to five, and reply.

Imagination may be more important than knowledge. I can know lots about myself and keep acting the same flawed way time and time again. But if I can imagine a different future that's attractive enough, then I just might find myself living in it. In my future, I see myself letting go those little annoyances I used to cling to, choosing instead to do battle over things that truly matter.

Today I'm pushing Nicholas's stroller across an intersection and chatting with Christine. Suddenly some idiot gabbing on a cell phone misses the red light and screeches to a stop, nearly running us over. I shout and yank the stroller out of the way while Christine pounds her hands on the hood—*bam bam bam*—and yells, "Watch it! You almost hit my baby!" As people stare, the driver has the gall to yell back at *us*, so Christine and I give the guy a tandem one-finger salute before continuing on our way, to the appreciative cheers and honks of the other drivers. Someone almost hit Nicholas—now *that's* something to be mad about! As we stride down the sidewalk, Christine and I turn toward each other and say at the same time, "Can you *believe* that guy?"

Most mornings, before I've had my second cup of coffee, I realize there's a lot to be mad at, starting with the front page of the paper and ending with the fact that I can't find my favorite sneakers. While some things deserve my anger, a lot of others don't, and all that extra emotion can boil inside of me. I'm scared of what I might do or say in anger; I want to be a healthy member of my family. What I cling to is the hope that I can choose a different path. It's easier to imagine living a different future when I've already pictured just how much better that future might be. When I get angry, it isn't in isolation. Christine and I are partners for life, and Nicholas is beginning to watch me, regardless of whether my anger is righteous or petty. I know I can't change overnight, but I also know I can't stay where I am. If I say a prayer—and squint my eyes—I can *just* make out a new path, sunlit and smooth, winding its way ahead.

Prayers

Nicholas jumped into prayer just like he jumps into any task that has discreet and repeatable parts, like opening and closing a door or turning a light on and off. It's easy: close eyes, hold hands—but only with Mom or Dad—shout out something to pray for—*babies! berries! cars!*—listen to Mom or Dad talk, yell "Amen!" and throw your hands up in the air like someone just kicked a field goal.

I'm hooked on these simple prayers. After sitting or snoring through three decades of long-winded discourses at church, school, and home, praying with Nicholas is refreshing. I've always put a lot of trust in the idea that God knows what I need—what I *really* need—even if I don't know myself, and that work done well is a form of prayer. But I can pray these baby prayers with Nicholas, no problem. I *get* them. It feels natural to help Nicholas talk to God about things that matter, like praying for the babies we saw at the park or being thankful for our tofu cubes. Nicholas and I can say, along with Anne Lamott, that our favorite prayers are "Help me, help me, help me" and "Thank you, thank you, thank you."

What worried me, though, is what would come next. If it's prayer today, then tomorrow it'll be Bible stories, sitting still in church, and trying to explain who Jesus is. Prayer is like a gateway drug that gets you hooked, and before you know it, you're into the hard stuff.

Sure enough, a little harmless praying and suddenly it was time to get Nicholas a children's Bible. It started with Nana, who bought him a hardback Bible and asked if she could read it with him. Christine and I both suffer from a severe allergy to Christian cheese, so we were afraid that it would be one of those kids' Bibles where Jesus looks like Rod Stewart with a neatly trimmed beard and the bad guys come straight from Disney's catalog of hook-nosed villains. But it didn't turn out to be *that* bad—a ringing compliment, for sure—and once Nicholas gets ahold of a new book, there's no turning back. Nicholas adores books, and when he learned that a Bible is a book with cool pictures and *lots* of stories from which he could choose, well, he was ready to answer the altar call. He even discovered that his Bible has a story about cars; it's clear to Nicholas that the treasure chest the third wise man is handing to baby Jesus is full of Hot Wheels.

Of course, once Nicholas started reading Bible stories before bed, I started feeling the urge to edit them. So what if the stories of the Bible have guided, inspired, and challenged people all over the world for thousands of years? Those same stories aren't quite right for *my* son. David and Bathsheba became a story about a lady swimming in a fun pool, and Absalom is playing a silly game up in a tree. What am I going to do when Nicholas can understand how *weird* these stories are? And how weird the people at church are?

For Christine and I, church has always been more than two-hours on Sunday. Our church is our extended family, so it's what we do all week, whether we're meeting at a friend's house to sing and pray on Wednesday night or taking a meal to a new mother. It also means going to church on Sunday, but there's nothing magical about that particular time. At least that's what we tell ourselves so we don't feel bad about how much we goof off during Sunday church.

Even before Nicholas was born, we both had trouble making it through the long prayers and sermons without doodling or writing funny notes to each other on the bulletin. Christine usually makes a to-do list for the week when the sermon starts, and I draw pictures of waves or think about something I want to write. Things have only gotten worse since we had Nicholas. His Bible stories each fit on one page with a nice full-color illustration. I mean, entire chapters of excruciatingly detailed instructions regarding the tabernacle are reduced to one page where the smiling Israelite workers make a colorful tent for God to live in; can you blame us for lacking the attention span to make it through a thirty-minute sermon? Maybe young parents should be allowed to go to a special service in which nothing lasts more than five minutes.

At his age, Nicholas goes to church with us by playing in the nursery. He doesn't know what Mommy and Daddy do in the big building across the street, but if he did, what would he think? When I walk down the aisle to take communion, I hear Nicholas's voice in my head saying, "Thank you for crackers, Jesus!" We make fun of all the spelling mistakes on the worship band's PowerPoint slides; we give each other back scratches. Are we going to have to cut out all the funny business and act like grown-ups when Nicholas sits beside us?

Teaching Nicholas about God feels like a really important task to me, one that I don't want to screw up. What we've experienced of God—love that doesn't quit, gentle restoration, firework flares of hope and courage—is too good *not* to want to pass on to Nicholas. For whatever reason, I feel like these first few years are so crucial, as if everything I do now will echo through the rest of Nicholas's life. Shouldn't someone more dependable be in charge here?

Recently, though, I reread in a letter something that put my daily decisions in perspective. Grandpa Robert Nicholas, my son's namesake, who died in 2000, wrote, "Fifty years from now you'll look back and see how the pattern of your lives fell into place as God led, even though it may seem a bit uncertain just now." If I could change the flow of time, I'd prefer to have Grandpa around to take over Nicholas's spiritual education, but short of that, I'm trying to trust what he wrote to me. Of course what I say to Nicholas matters, but I shouldn't get too far ahead of myself. Nicholas isn't even two, and we've got a lot more life together. Besides, what I do will surely teach Nicholas more than what I say, a frightening conclusion on its own.

It's time for me to take a deep breath and try to believe that I'll be okay, and that Nicholas will be, too. The love that is God doesn't depend on which Bible stories I read my son before bed. And yet, wonderfully, some of God's love *does* live on in those stories we read together and in the prayers we say at bedtime. I turn out the lights and settle Nicholas on my lap. "Let's say our prayers," I tell him, and almost before I finish my sentence, he's off and running: "Mommy Daddy Nicholas Kim Lena …"

I gently interrupt him. "Okay, honey, let's pray for all the people we love."

"All people," Nicholas agrees, scrunching his eyelids and forehead like he's staring at the sun.

"Dear Jesus," I say.

"Dear Jesus," he repeats.

"Thank you for Mommy," I begin.

"Thank you Mommy, Nana, Papa, Sam, Jamie, Papa Doug, Mama Sherrill, Nicholas, Mama, Daddy, Kim, Lena, Nicholas . . ."

He seems like he'll continue in this vein for quite a while, so I gently interrupt him again. "Amen," I say and hug him.

He looks up at me like he's wondering why I didn't let him pray for everyone on his list. "And Mommy Daddy Nicholas," he adds. "Amen!"

As we circle the room to say goodnight to things, Nicholas wants me to open the closet door. Inside the closet, on top of his dresser, there is a small wooden triptych of St. Nicholas given to him by his great-aunt Jean. I open its fragile wings for him, and he touches each of them while he whispers his name over and over. Beside the triptych is a photograph of Grandpa Nicholas and me. In the photo, I am three years old and Grandpa is reading me a bedtime story. I have on pajamas and a baseball hat. Nicholas takes the picture from the dresser and looks at it. "Night, Papa Bob; love you," he says. He tries to put the picture back on the dresser, but it clatters onto its side, and as I stand it up, Nicholas turns his hands palms-up in a gesture of uncertainty. "Where Papa Bob?" "He's right here," I tell Nicholas, handing him the picture again. Nicholas once more sets the picture down, looks around the room, and asks, "Where Papa Bob?"

Suddenly I get it. The question goes straight inside me. It feels like a cup of sadness and longing has been poured out in my chest, and I can feel the bittersweet liquid slowly filling my body. "Do you want to see Papa Bob?" I ask Nicholas, my face inches from his. "Nicholas see Papa Bob?" he answers, his voice rising in hope. "Oh, honey," I breathe, my forehead touching his now. "Play cars Papa Bob?" asks Nicholas. My cup runs over, still pouring out as I hold Nicholas as close to me as I can. "I hope so, little one," I tell him. "He'd love that."

Love, Grown-up Style

I used to be pretty carefree, but then I became a father. Some of my worries seem legitimate: Is Nicholas growing like he should? What are we teaching him? What is he learning by watching me? Some, however, are purely the product of neurosis. Why does Nicholas have fewer teeth than our friends' child who is three months younger? How high will gas prices be when he starts to drive? New dads don't have a place to talk about this kind of stuff. I recently learned about stitch-and-bitch groups and I felt envious. I imagined myself sitting around with a few other dads talking about our fears and frustrations while knitting. Really, though, we'd probably be watching a basketball game. And not talking.

I already had experience with guy groups that work less than perfectly. When Christine was in her third trimester, we attended a prenatal parent workshop at our hospital. After a promising start—there was a donut shop in the lobby—things headed south. The nurse in charge corralled the unwilling men into a circle so that we could have a sharing time. Under normal circumstances, a group of random guys needs an activity to induce conversation, like a watching a movie or an attractive woman strolling past, and this wasn't even close to normal circumstances.

As we sat there, checking our watches and seeing who could slouch the lowest in his chair, our wives across the room were in full-scale girlfriend mode, laughing and crying with equal gusto. I found myself the unwilling leader of our sorry circle, trying to drag answers out of the other dads. (Me: "So ... does anyone want to share what they're feeling?" Tall Guy: "Um, I guess I feel, uh, scared." Me: "What do you feel scared of?" Tall Guy: "Y'know, becoming a dad and stuff." Me: "Hold on, let me write that on our whiteboard.") It looked like it would be up to me, myself, and I to deal with whatever issues came up.

One particular worry gnawed at me more than the others during Christine's pregnancy, and it dug in and hung on well into the first few months of Nicholas's life. This concern wasn't one that I could communicate easily to other people, partly because I didn't understand it myself, and partly because it seemed stupid when I verbalized it. Will Christine, I wondered, love me less after our baby is born?

This fear did come up in conversation occasionally, but each time I was handed pat answers. When you have a baby, people told me, the love in your family expands; you'll have even more love than you did when it was just the two of you! Hogwash, I thought. Either Christine will be holding the baby, or she'll be holding me. It can't be both, and I bet I'll lose out.

In the weeks after Nicholas was born, I suspected that I'd been right. He seemed ready to replace me. I could see the attraction: he was attentive, clean shaven, and ready to cuddle at the drop of a diaper. Nicholas didn't have many other social engagements, so he and his mom spent a lot of time together, eating, sleeping, bonding, and generally going gaga for each other. Meanwhile, Christine and I began to relate more mechanically, both physically and emotionally. Each change reinforced the other: since we were tired, we had less energy for conversation and support, and since we were talking less, our physical gestures began to wither. In the absence of anyone to tell me differently, I figured that this was the way things went. Long hugs were replaced by short, tentative ones, so as not to hurt Christine's tender nursing boobs. Conversations revolved around baby poop and feeding charts.

When Nicholas was less than a week old, Christine and I left him with his grandma Sherrill and went out on a date. We had planned to do this because we knew that couples need time to themselves after having a baby, and this was the perfect chance, since it was Christine's birthday. We sat across the table from each other in a cozy booth at our local diner. I felt excited: I was already on a date! That meant that Nicholas wasn't totally ruling things. I felt proud. How many other dads could say that they'd been out for a relaxing dinner with their wife less than a week after their child was born? What I hadn't planned was Christine bursting into tears soon after we sat down. I sat in stunned silence. Was this the postpartum depression I'd heard about? Was this how things were going to be? As she excused herself to the washroom, I stared at the table, arranging and rearranging the silverware.

As the days turned into weeks, and the weeks into months, we began to figure out what life as a family looked like. We took walks together, and I learned how to play peekaboo with Nicholas in the stroller. We learned how to have conversations while warming up bottles and bouncing a baby on our hips. Christine discovered a game called Where's the Baby? that's as much fun for the spectators as it is for the participants. She hoists Nicholas into the air, balancing his chubby tummy on the top of her head, after which she runs around the room shouting, "Where's the baby? Where's the baby?" as Nicholas is reduced to helpless laughter. His legs and head bounce fore and aft of Christine's head, and he clutches handfuls of her hair like a cowboy hanging on to the saddle horn while riding a bucking horse.

As I lived the life of a dad, I found that the routine of daily life became more and more comfortable. There were fewer times that I compared my current life to my life before Nicholas, though waking up at 6:00 AM on Saturday was still a downer. And it was in the context of learning that my current life is the only life I can live that moments of deep goodness broke through like shoots of grass through cracks in the sidewalk.

One such moment happened when Nicholas was about a year old. I was sitting on the floor playing with him. Or, more accurately, I was in the same room as Nicholas, and he was playing while I was watching a basketball game. He's learned that Dad usually has a belt on and that belts are fascinating. He pulled up my shirt and laughed when he saw my belt. He tugged on the end of it and laughed when it snapped back again. I said something automatic—*Oh, you found Daddy's belt*—and kept watching. This night, though, Nicholas noticed that above Dad's belt is Dad's stomach. Perhaps some neurons finally made a connection in his growing brain—Dad tickles *my* stomach—or perhaps it was just a lark. For whatever reason, Nicholas gave my stomach a two-handed tickle that caught me off-guard. It really tickled! I let out a guffaw and looked at Nicholas, who was staring at me with a look of flat-out delight: *I made*

Daddy laugh! I turned the television off and gave my full attention to the fun of being Nicholas's dad.

The other morning I lay in bed with Christine. Nicholas was between us, drinking his bottle and looking at the white Christmas lights that are strung above our bed. I said, "Good morning, hon." Christine replied with a muffled "Morning," her face still buried in her pillow. I craned my head over Nicholas and his bottle to give her a good-morning kiss, the kind of sleepy peck that we're used to. That morning, though, for some reason, I noticed how real Christine is—how warm and soft and physically near me. My best friend and lover sleeps in the same bed as me every night—what are the odds! With Nicholas squeezed between us and happily sucking on his bottle, I kept my head on Christine's side of the bed and traced the curve of her nose with the tip of mine. I kissed her again, and she kissed me back. In that kiss—with our horrible morning breath, our tousled hair, our drool-stained pillows, and our drinking baby sandwiched between us—we remembered each other. We breathed life into each other's tired limbs. We glimpsed for a moment the unmeasured depths below the surface of our love.

I'm so used to living with Christine that I forget to pay attention to what motivates her. When we first got married, I knew that the salmon dinner she fixed me was an expression of how much she loved me. Now, almost six years into our marriage, I've become so used to Christine's love that I take her actions for granted. I can taste the salmon without remembering why she bothered to cook it for me. Now that we're raising Nicholas, though, I get to peer behind the scenes. Nicholas is oblivious to so much of what goes on in our home that it's almost comical. He's a creature of the moment. He wants his favorite toy or bottle or whatever, *right now!* He doesn't know that Christine plans out his menus several meals in advance, rotates his toys, washes and folds his clothes, monitors his diaper rash over the course of a week, talks with me about his sleep patterns and how to improve them, and generally makes sure that he has every opportunity to be happy and well. At least one of the Jacobsen men is paying attention, though. I know that her actions have the weight of love behind them. She wants Nicholas to grow bigger and stronger, to have fun, to feel safe and loved, and to learn boundaries. He knows nothing of these intentions. For him, her actions are enough. For me, seeing the inside of Christine's love for Nicholas helps me experience Christine's love for me in a new way.

Recently I had a vision, the kind of experience during which it feels like time stops for a moment and a choir sings while a shaft of sunlight shines down on the scene. The object of my vision was Christine's right forearm and hand. I see and touch Christine every day, but on this occasion I actually saw her. We were sitting side by side in church. I looked down and saw that her arm and hand were powerful and strong. I could see muscles slightly tensed just below the surface of her skin. The outline of a vein ran like a wire along the top of her forearm, disappearing into the back of her hand. The thin tendons connecting her knuckles and wrist stood slightly raised, ready for action. Her skin was both older and more beautiful. I'm used to viewing Christine's body as athletic as I watch her run and play soccer. But this was something else. Her arm, toned and muscled, was now more than a means to excel at sports. It was, instead, strong in service to another. It was a mother's arm. It was the sort of capable, strong arm that carries children, lugs backpacks, and hoists shopping bags. It had the sort of strength that restrains itself, that brushes hair, wipes noses, and ties shoelaces. As I looked at her arm, I loved it, as strange as that sounds. I knew that I wanted to feel that arm around my waist for the rest of my life. I knew that I need to hold exactly that particular hand, my fingers interlaced in hers, as we walk together toward the next thing.

Rookie Dad

I'll confess something. Sometimes, when I'm barreling along on the highway, I think about what it would be like to jerk the wheel to the left and swerve into oncoming traffic. I tell myself that I won't actually *do* it, and that I can't be the only one who has that sort of thought. If you notice that Christine does all the driving from here on out, you'll know why. Lately, though, I've felt like other drivers are trying to swerve into *me*, and I don't like it. I don't mean real drivers, but expectations as big as eighteen-wheelers. I'm trying to mind my own business—driving in a straight line and keeping my family safe—and now I have to worry about expectations that have the pedal to the metal and an evil glint in their eyes.

It's an ordinary evening. The highway is clear and smooth, but there are headlights in the distance. I'm checking email in our bedroom. Christine looks at me with a sheepish smile. "I have some pictures to show you, okay?"

"Okaaay," I reply, wondering what's in store for me. Perhaps after regaining her trim figure after Nicholas's birth, Christine has taken some racy pictures of herself in lingerie. We've both been making an effort lately to get back in shape, after all. I'm certain that my always attractive figure is even more desirable now that I can run for at least twenty-five minutes without stopping to hurl. Maybe I should take some pictures for *her*, since she's taken these for me.

Christine stands beside me as iPhoto loads, her hand resting lightly on my shoulder. My fantasy ends abruptly. Instead of Sexy Christine, the screen is filled with the image of my son, Nicholas. Wearing an oh-so-cute turquoise dress. Did I mention that my son is a boy?

If I try to ignore temporarily my various hang-ups and insecurities, it's really quite a charming picture. I'm the first one to wax eloquent about how beautiful Nicholas is, and he's at the top of his game in this picture. Nicholas is at the age when showing off is one of his main goals. In this instance, as Christine told me, he was able to show off for both Mom *and* Auntie Lisa *and* the camera at the same time. There he is, captured midtwirl. The dress is swirling lightly from his shoulders, rotating back in the direction of his spin. His arms are outstretched, delicately downward, while a giant grin lights up his face. It is the perfect picture of my son in a dress. And I hate it.

I like to indulge in some Psych 101-isms every once in a while: So, you are a young father upset by the sight of your young son in a dress, eh? Clearly you are under the impression that the way your son dresses and behaves reflects on his masculinity and, therefore, on your own. Perhaps you are afraid that he will grow up to be a bit of a—how shall we put it?—a dandy? Young man, are you afraid of being a father? Is this really about your own sexual insecurities? Or your own sexual desires? Perhaps you do not feel like a real man. Your father may have something to do with this, and your mother, too. I want you to think about these things, but don't rush it. I'm sure we will have many interesting sessions together, you and I.

I'm sure. It's funny how much credence I give the German-accented fogey in my head, even though I made him up. What's the big deal about Nicholas wearing a blue dress, anyway? In my head, I know what the answer is: nothing. No big deal. But I see all those questions the dress stirs up—all those insecurities and doubts and fears—as the lights of an oncoming truck. Do I let those questions run me over? What will happen if I swerve? And what ever happened to the simple road of parenting a newborn—eat, change, swaddle, set the cruise control, and try to stay awake?

It's not just strange events—like my wife dressing my son up like a girl—that screw with me, either. It's normal, everyday stuff, like going for a walk with my family. When we stroll around our neighborhood, I usually invite Envy along for company. Envy's great to bring because he always has something to say about the houses, cars, dogs, and various domestic accouterments we pass. He asks me if I realize that owning a house would make me the happiest, most fulfilled man in the world. I usually sigh before agreeing. Why can't I take a different Deadly Sin with me? Gluttony would be perfect, since I could walk off the weight at the same time I was gaining it. As I near thirty, though, I'm beginning to suspect that we don't get to pick our vices. They pick us, I think, and stick around through thick and thin.

And it's not all happy talk with Envy, either. He can be a real prick when he brings up the whole emasculating I'm-not-providing-for-my-family thing. We're young, I tell him, still finding our way through various changes and transitions, and so far we haven't lacked anything that matters. He tells me to stuff the hippie talk and start being a man. Get on the path to success, he says—don't your wife and kid deserve the best? Name one of your friends, he demands, who's less of a man than you are! When we get home from our walk, I'm going to make a serious effort to look up Gluttony's number and invite him along next time.

I read enough to know that, according to almost everyone—economists, philosophers, preachers, sociologists, and so on—having more stuff doesn't mean that I'll be happier or more of a man or a better dad. The trouble is that the people who think that more is always better have a really big megaphone and they're not afraid to use it. If I want to be a better dad, why should I work harder on my relationships with my family or practice self-examination or join a woodworking class when I can just buy Nicholas a new train set online? As much as I hate to admit it, I get run over by this lie all the time; I'm so used to being flattened that I can hardly remember what it's like to stand up straight.

What scares me is the notion that I might pass this handicap on to Nicholas, or that it's being inextricably woven into him from day one, like a rough, brown thread through a delicate white cloth. Christine and I have a favorite store slogan, one we learned while we were deciding where to register for Nicholas's baby shower. Babies "R" Us (thankfully my computer doesn't know how to participate in the inane reversing of the "R") offers its customers the following pearl of wisdom regarding babies: "For being so little, they sure need a lot."

Of *course* they do, we laugh, as long as all of it comes from *your* store, right? Sure, human babies have survived fairly well for a decently long time with just a few essentials: warmth, milk, care, and some sort of fun toy, like a stick or a rock. However, according to the baby industry, humans now seem to have entered an evolutionary stage in which a baby won't survive unless that baby sleeps in a crib with a bumper pad that matches the sheets and has fifteen blankets of different thicknesses, an electric wipe warmer, and the Diaper Buddy 9000—and that's just the bare minimum. Next month's catalog will tell you what else you need.

Okay, okay, I'll come clean. Nicholas *does* have a bumper pad in his crib that matches his sheets. And a wall hanging to go with it. And maybe a lamp, too, but that's all! It's not like we bought into the store slogan or anything. It's more accurate to say that our generous family and friends bought us into it. By the time we unwrapped gifts from three different baby showers, we felt like we were preparing for the arrival of six babies instead of one. Before Christine was pregnant, I figured that babies would kind of lounge around in some sort of shapeless pink or blue outfit until turning two, at which point they would hop into a pair of jeans or a dress from Sears in size XXS. However, I can now report to you— and I swear this is true—that when Nicholas was born, he had a dresser waiting for him at home with more clothes in it than *I* owned. And this, mind you, didn't include the two huge boxes of extra clothes under his crib or the fancy clothes in his closet. I certainly don't feel good about Nicholas's having all those things, partly because it makes me realize that we're part of the system, and partly because it makes me realize how much I own that I don't need. How am I going to teach Nicholas to be content with enough instead of with more when *I'm* not content with enough?

A few weeks ago I was in one of those weepy reflective moods that hit me at night and I don't mention during the day. I was telling Nicholas some Important Things as he sat on my lap drinking his bottle. Most of it doesn't concern anyone else, but for the purposes of this story, I need to tell you that I said this to him: "You're just a little guy now, but as you grow up, I'm going to teach you how to be a man."

Every so often I make a statement that's so preposterous my own words seem to slap me in the face like the end of a whip, like when I shout at Christine during an argument, "No, *you're* being unreasonable!" I'm going to teach you how to be a man, huh? Is that right after I teach you how to breathe underwater? I was glad that it was dark and that Nicholas was more interested in his milk than in my words, glad that for a least a few more years, he wouldn't notice anything out of place in my promise. Glad, too, that I could backpedal from that kind of parental promise before Nicholas's adolescent BS detector becomes fully operational and he pays more attention to my failures than my intentions.

What changed my mood from self-pity to full-scale freak-out was the realization that I *would* keep that promise, every day for the rest of my life, and there was nothing that Nicholas or I could do about it, however much one of us might want to. I'm going to teach you how to be a man, whether you like it or not, little guy. And through that one flawed lesson you're going to extrapolate how to be a husband and a friend, and you're going to grope for what it means when you hear that God is your father. The rocking chair was getting crowded: me, my son, and my fears, rocking back and forth. I shivered as the thermostat kicked in and the heater turned on again.

As I write this, I study the picture of Nicholas in a blue dress, careful, of course, not to let anyone else at The Daily Grind coffee shop see what I'm looking at. It's true—he looks adorable. And given the wonders of genetics, it may very well be that a future daughter of mine could look much the same at that young age. Imagining that future picture, I think that I will be delighted by the way her dress flows in a circle as she twirls, just as I tell myself that I can, and should, be delighted in the way my son looks. I mean, would I like things any better if I'd dressed him up in overalls and work boots and put a hard hat on his head? Or if he were holding a toy rifle and wearing fatigues? Would that be more manly, more in keeping with what I want him to be? With what I want myself to be?

I've never quite fit the stereotype of the Great American Male; on a college trip to England I was voted most likely to become the next Romantic poet, for goodness' sake! This is a lousy time to try to figure out what it means to be a man, considering the dysfunctional models that my country and my religion offer me. I should be strong and bold, ready to kill bad guys and buy a new truck with equal ease. My house is my castle and my thoughts are my own. I'm an army of one, righteous and confident and so smoothly shaven that my wife can't keep her hands off me. My theology and politics are all right —how about yours? Now that you mention it, my new flat screen *is* bigger than yours, but don't worry, I still give to charity. Haven't you heard? The world's black and white, left and right, and *I* know where *I* stand.

Except that I don't. Too bad doubt isn't manly, or frustration with the status quo, or insecurity. If wanting to scream almost every time I leaf through the paper or watch television or think about raising Nicholas made me manly, well, then, you could call me Johnny Rambo.

When careless words recoil, they cut like a whip, but sometimes careless words can yield unexpected insight.

Remembering what I said to Nicholas, I thought, *About all I know for sure about being a man is that I have a penis!* Well duh! But then I realized that I had a pretty good point. By virtue of having a penis, I'm a man, and that biological truth led to my marriage to Christine, which led to my having a child who is also a man, a child who already knows that he and Daddy are boys and Mommy is a girl. So maybe that's as good a place to start as any. Maybe I can promise to teach Nicholas how to be a man when I understand that being a man isn't a set of beliefs or actions but something that you are and that you become. He *is* a man already, albeit one who is less than three feet tall and who laughs whenever he hears the word *poop*. And he'll *become* a man every day of his life as he chooses how to act and think and live. Whether I like it or not, I'll be the biggest single influence on Nicholas's growth as a man. Come to think of it, I guess it's already happening, since I laugh whenever I hear the word *poop*, too.

Nicholas and I read a book together called *Going to Work*. Cute little construction workers show up to their job site and get to work. I like to change the words a bit, though. To "knock down that building" I add "so we can make a new mixed-income housing project," and to "bulldoze that tree" I add "so that we can plant a drought-friendly garden." The workers don't dump their rubble; they recycle it. The smiles on the workers' faces lead me to think that they agree with my changes. But Nicholas is his own man already. Since he can't read, he falls for my storytelling propaganda. When he plays with his favorite toy, though, I can't help but cringe: it's a Cadillac Escalade. I resolutely refused to call it an SUV for a few weeks, but Nicholas won out. He calls it his "really big SUV," and now I do, too. But nothing can get in the way of my love for Nicholas—not even an Escalade. He's still my little guy. As he grows up, I won't stop loving him for any other reason, either, even if he wants to start wearing dresses. I guess that means that I've committed myself to teaching him what it means to be a man after all. Next time I put Nicholas to bed, I'll tell him that being a man means loving each other as we become whatever we are meant to be. It means loving across gaps and when we're not sure. I'll whisper lines from Madeleine L'Engle's "The Woman" to him:

> only in the is
> (not the ought)
> can love grow.

Knowing him, he'll probably burp, and both of us will laugh in the dark.

What's the best gift that I can give Nicholas? Given my current career, it doesn't look like handing him a pile of material riches will be an option, tempting though it is to think of wealth as the universal problem-solver.

But if not wealth, then what? I think I can already guess at the answer. If there's one thing I know, it's this: Even though I'm just a rookie now, I'll be Nicholas's dad for the rest of his life. Neither of us will get pulled from the game. I'm the starting dad for Team Jacobsen, and God willing, we've got a long season ahead of us.

So Nicholas, the next time Envy comes on our family walk, I promise to stick my fingers in my ears and hum; maybe he'll shut his cake hole for once. I promise that I'll do my best to make sure that you always have enough, whatever enough looks like for our family; we'll have to discover it as we go. When you're older, it might mean that you'll ask me to give a pair of my running shoes to a homeless guy who hangs out by your school, since yours won't fit him; maybe you'll decide that planting a new garden is the birthday present you *really* want. *Maybe* it means that I'll buy you a battery-powered Escalade for you to drive around in on your third birthday, but boy-oh-boy, do I hope not! No matter what shape our love takes, Son, I promise you this: as the season goes by, we'll work on our game together.

Pretty-Pretty

It's Sunday afternoon, and Christine and I take Nicholas for a hike in the University Endowment Lands. Miraculously, this two-thousand-acre swath of forest has escaped the hyperdevelopment that characterizes nearly all of greater Vancouver. It's no work at all to leave the city and plunge into a green world of towering firs, cedars, and red maples. Squirrels, coyotes, hawks, and eagles make their homes here right next door to booming subdivisions and business districts. A short walk, and the branches swallow the sounds of cars and busses.

Today it is cool and misty, a kind of half-fog, half-cloud that's common in Vancouver. We push, cram, and strap Nicholas into our hiking backpack, a process which he hates. Each time I tighten a buckle, he says, "Uh*ahh!*" and jerks his limbs to let us know he isn't happy. But once I heft him onto my back, he loves it; suddenly, he's six feet tall!

We cross the street and enter the forest, and as the city sounds fade behind us, the fog thickens, spinning and swirling between the tall trunks. Christine strides beside me on the packed gravel path, our running shoes crunching in sync. Our conversation is focused—what will the next year of our lives look like?—but it's hard to stay focused in this environment. Our sentences are cut off: *If you work mornings and I work nights, then ... Oh! Look at that nurse log—it must be five feet thick!*

The path forks around a large fir tree. I give a conspiratorial stage whisper over my shoulder to Nicholas: "Let's go surprise Mom!" Nicholas knows that when we whisper like this, something funny is about to happen. As we trot ahead and hide behind the tree, he can't contain himself, and he begins to giggle. I can feel his body shaking with delight. "Shh!" I remind him. "We're surprising Mom!" This elicits more giggles. A second later, I jump out from behind the tree, and Nicholas guffaws as Mom mock-screams in surprise. Nicholas lets out a long sigh, which I interpret: *Ahh, that was a good one, Dad.*

For most of the hike it's easy to remember that Nicholas is on my back. He kicks his legs, waves his arms, yells out "Doggie! Doggie!" when joggers and their dogs trot past, and chomps on crackers right in my ear. But there are moments when the three of us are silent, and the only sound is our footsteps and the steady puffs of our breath that hang as fog within the fog.

As we hike in momentary silence, I glimpse in my peripheral vision a striped mitten reaching for the trailing branches of a Western red cedar. Christine and I both stop, and now the only sound is the patter of water falling all around us. We can smell this cedar tree, pungent and sharp. Its lower branches stoop toward the path. Its leaves, which overlap each other like the scales of a snake, are an unusually bright green that seems to glow in the dim light. At the tip of each leaf, droplets of shining water hang like tiny fruit. Nicholas reaches out his mittened hand and gently pets the cedar leaves—once, twice, three times. Behind me, in my right ear, I hear his husky whisper: "Pretty-pretty, pretty-pretty."

We continue hiking, stopping now and again to examine more pretty-prettys. Nicholas names other dogs and eats more crackers. Christine and I get partway through planning our life; we'll take another hike next weekend. I don't know a lot about being a dad, and I can't predict what sort of young man Nicholas will grow up to be. But I guess if he knows that a cedar cloaked in dew is pretty-pretty, then he's off to a good start. And so, for the moment, am I.

Acknowledgments

Thank you to everyone who read drafts of this book, especially Maxine Hancock and Nicola Aimé. Without you, *Rookie Dad* might still exist, but it would be really, really bad.

Thank you to my editors at Zondervan, Angela Scheff and Brian Phipps, who gave me daily reasons to pull out what remains of my hair.

Thank you to Richard, Elaine, Doug, and Sherrill for support that's way above and far beyond.

Thank you to Nicholas for learning to sleep through the night, and for laughing at my jokes.

Thank you to Christine for not laughing when I wrote you that sonnet when we were freshman, or when I told you that I wanted to be a writer.

Thank you to my local coffee shop, The Daily Grind, for letting me write every day for the price of a mug of Peruvian Vibration.

We want to hear from you. Please send your comments about this book to us in care of zreview@zondervan.com. Thank you.

ZONDERVAN.com/
AUTHORTRACKER
follow your favorite authors